Relations between Precipitation, Groundwater Withdrawals, and Changes in Hydrologic Conditions at Selected Monitoring Sites in Volusia County, Florida, 1995–2010

By Louis C. Murray, Jr.

Prepared in cooperation with the
St. Johns River Water Management District

Scientific Investigations Report 2012–5075

U.S. Department of the Interior
U.S. Geological Survey

U.S. Department of the Interior
KEN SALAZAR, Secretary

U.S. Geological Survey
Marcia K. McNutt, Director

U.S. Geological Survey, Reston, Virginia: 2012

For more information on the USGS—the Federal source for science about the Earth, its natural and living resources, natural hazards, and the environment, visit *http://www.usgs.gov* or call 1–888–ASK–USGS.

For an overview of USGS information products, including maps, imagery, and publications, visit *http://www.usgs.gov/pubprod*

To order this and other USGS information products, visit *http://store.usgs.gov*

Suggested citation:
Murray, L.C., Jr., 2012, Relations between precipitation, groundwater withdrawals, and changes in hydrologic conditions at selected monitoring sites in Volusia County, Florida, 1995–2010: U.S. Geological Survey Scientific Investigations Report 2012–5075, 43 p. (Also available at *http://pubs.usgs.gov/sir/2012/5075/*.)

Contents

Figures

Tables

Conversion Factors and Datums

Inch/Pound to SI

Multiply	By	To obtain
Length		
inch (in.)	2.54	centimeter (cm)
foot (ft)	0.3048	meter (m)
mile (mi)	1.609	kilometer (km)
Flow		
foot per month (ft/mo)	0.3048	meter per month (m/mo)
cubic foot per second (ft³/s)	0.02832	cubic meter per second (m³/s)
million gallons per day (Mgal/d)	0.04381	cubic meters per second (m³/s)
inch per month (in/mo)	25.4	millimeter per month (mm/mo)
inch per year (in/yr)	25.4	millimeter per year (mm/yr)

Vertical coordinate information is referenced to the National Geodetic Vertical Datum of 1929 (NGVD 29).

Horizontal coordinate information is referenced to the North American Datum of 1983 (NAD 83).

Altitude, as used in this report, refers to distance above the vertical datum.

Abbreviations and Acronyms

FAS	Floridan aquifer system
FDEP	Florida Department of Environmental Protection
GIS	geographic information system
ICU	intermediate confining unit
LFA	Lower Floridan aquifer
MFL	minimum flows and levels
MLR	multiple linear regression
MSCU	middle semiconfining unit
NOAA	National Oceanic and Atmospheric Administration
PET	potential evapotranspiration
POR	period of record
R^2	coefficient of determination
R^2_{adj}	adjusted coefficient of determination
SAS	surficial aquifer system
SIV	stressor influence value
SJRWMD	St. Johns River Water Management District
UFA	Upper Floridan aquifer
USGS	U.S. Geological Survey
VIF	variance inflation factor

Relations between Precipitation, Groundwater Withdrawals, and Changes in Hydrologic Conditions at Selected Monitoring Sites in Volusia County, Florida, 1995–2010

By Louis C. Murray, Jr.

Abstract

A study to examine the influences of climatic and anthropogenic stressors on groundwater levels, lake stages, and surface-water discharge at selected sites in northern Volusia County, Florida, was conducted in 2009 by the U.S. Geological Survey. Water-level data collected at 20 monitoring sites (17 groundwater and 3 lake sites) in the vicinity of a wetland area were analyzed with multiple linear regression to examine the relative influences of precipitation and groundwater withdrawals on changes in groundwater levels and lake stage. Analyses were conducted across varying periods of record between 1995 and 2010 and included the effects of groundwater withdrawals aggregated from municipal water-supply wells located within 12 miles of the project sites. Surface-water discharge data at the U.S. Geological Survey Tiger Bay canal site were analyzed for changes in flow between 1978 and 2001.

As expected, water-level changes in monitoring wells located closer to areas of concentrated groundwater withdrawals were more highly correlated with withdrawals than were water-level changes measured in wells further removed from municipal well fields. Similarly, water-level changes in wells tapping the Upper Floridan aquifer, the source of municipal supply, were more highly correlated with groundwater withdrawals than were water-level changes in wells tapping the shallower surficial aquifer system. Water-level changes predicted by the regression models over precipitation-averaged periods of record were underestimated for observations having large positive monthly changes (generally greater than 1.0 foot). Such observations are associated with high precipitation and were identified as points in the regression analyses that produced large standardized residuals and/or observations of high influence. Thus, regression models produced by multiple linear regression analyses may have better predictive capability in wetland environments when applied to periods of average or below average precipitation conditions than during wetter than average conditions.

For precipitation-averaged hydrologic conditions, water-level changes in the surficial aquifer system were statistically correlated solely with precipitation or were more highly correlated with precipitation than with groundwater withdrawals. Changes in Upper Floridan aquifer water levels and in water-surface stage (stage) at Indian and Scoggin Lakes tended to be highly correlated with both precipitation and withdrawals. The greater influence of withdrawals on stage changes, relative to changes in nearby surficial aquifer system water levels, indicates that these karstic lakes may be better connected hydraulically with the underlying Upper Floridan aquifer than is the surficial aquifer system at the other monitoring sites. At most sites, and for both aquifers, the 2-month moving average of precipitation or groundwater withdrawals included as an explanatory variable in the regression models indicates that water-level changes are not only influenced by stressor conditions across the current month, but also by those of the previous month.

The relations between changes in water levels, precipitation, and groundwater withdrawals varied seasonally and in response to a period of drought. Water-level changes tended to be most highly correlated with withdrawals during the spring, when relatively large increases contributed to water-level declines, and during the fall when reduced withdrawal rates contributed to water-level recovery. Water-level changes tended to be most highly (or solely) correlated with precipitation in the winter, when withdrawals are minimal, and in the summer when precipitation is greatest. Water-level changes measured during the drought of October 2005 to June 2008 tended to be more highly correlated with groundwater withdrawals at Upper Floridan aquifer sites than at surficial aquifer system sites, results that were similar to those for precipitation-averaged conditions. Also, changes in stage at Indian and Scoggin Lakes were highly correlated with precipitation and groundwater withdrawals during the drought. Groundwater-withdrawal rates during the drought were, on average, greater than those for precipitation-averaged conditions.

Accounting only for withdrawals aggregated from pumping wells located within varying radial distances of less than 12 miles of each site produced essentially the same relation between water-level changes and groundwater withdrawals as that determined for withdrawals aggregated within 12 miles of the site. Similarly, increases in withdrawals aggregated over distances of 1 to 12 miles of the sites had little effect on adjusted R-squared values.

Analyses of streamflow measurements collected between 1978 and 2001 at the U.S. Geological Survey Tiger Bay canal site indicate that significant changes occurred during base-flow conditions during that period. Hypothesis and trend testing, together with analyses of flow duration, the number of zero-flow days, and double-mass curves indicate that, after 1988, when a municipal well field began production, base flow was statistically lower than the period before 1988. This decrease in base flow could not be explained by variations in precipitation between these two periods.

Introduction

Most of the potable water used for municipal, agricultural, commercial, and industrial supply in east-central Florida is pumped from the Floridan aquifer system (FAS), a semi-confined sequence of highly transmissive carbonate rocks. Withdrawals from this system not only lower water levels, which can adversely affect the discharge from Upper Floridan aquifer (UFA) springs, but can also lower water levels in the overlying surficial aquifer system (SAS). Lowered SAS water levels, in turn, can affect other sensitive water resources, such as wetlands and associated ecosystems. In addition to groundwater withdrawals, natural climatic variables, such as precipitation and evapotranspiration, influence groundwater levels and affect water resources; however, it is often not apparent how these factors contribute to changes in SAS and UFA water levels. Consequently, trends and fluctuations observed in hydrologic data can reflect the combined effects of both climatic and anthropogenic influences and thus pose difficulties for water-resource managers tasked with assessing the impacts of groundwater withdrawals on wetlands or other hydrologic conditions.

Multiple linear regression (MLR) is a statistical tool that can be used to identify measureable properties or parameters (such as groundwater withdrawal and precipitation) that explain the variability observed in some property or parameter

(such as groundwater levels) of interest to resource managers. The MLR tool has been used in at least two previous USGS studies to examine the influences of groundwater withdrawals and precipitation on UFA water levels in central Florida (Lopez and Fretwell, 1992; Murray, 2010). Additional applications, however, are needed to better evaluate the applicability and limitations of MLR in helping to assess loss or expansion of wetland areas, such as those in northern Volusia County, due to groundwater withdrawals or climate effects (fig. 1). The northern part of Volusia County provides a suitable location for further development and testing of the MLR tool because the wetlands in this area are located near municipal water-supply well fields, and because sufficient and varied hydrologic data are available for analyses. In addition, three lakes in the area (Indian Lake, Coon Pond, and Scoggin Lake) have been designated by the St. Johns River Water Management District (SJRWMD) as "minimum flows and level" (MFL) lakes. MFLs are the minimum water flows and water-surface levels adopted by the SJRWMD Governing Board as necessary to prevent significant harm to the water resources or ecology of an area resulting from permitted withdrawals. Given the nature of the wetland conditions (the presence of low-lying areas situated within a surface-water basin of low gradient), the presence of nearby well fields, and the availability of hydrologic and water-use information, the U.S. Geological Survey (USGS), in cooperation with the SJRWMD, initiated a 2¼-year study in 2009 to examine the influences of climatic and anthropogenic stressors on groundwater levels, lake stages, and surface-water discharge at selected sites in northern Volusia County.

Purpose and Scope

This report presents the results of a study designed to assess the relative influences of precipitation and groundwater withdrawals on groundwater levels, lake levels, and on changes in streamflow at selected monitoring sites located within a wetland area of northern Volusia County. Water-level data collected at 17 groundwater sites and the 3 MFL lakes were analyzed using MLR across varying periods of record between 1995 and 2010. Streamflow data collected from a nearby USGS canal gaging station were analyzed using flow duration and double-mass curves, trend testing, and hypothesis testing to identify changes in flow conditions between 1978 and 2001. Results are used to test how effectively the MLR tool, in addition to other statistical tools used in the surface-water analyses, can be applied to identify and describe the effects of groundwater withdrawals and climate variability on wetland conditions that may be applicable in similar Florida settings.

Climatic variables of interest in this study included precipitation and potential evapotranspiration (PET), which can be defined as the amount of water that can be removed by the atmosphere from a free water surface (such as a lake) by evaporation and transpiration, assuming no limit on the surface-water supply. Municipal groundwater withdrawal is the anthropogenic variable tested in these relations.

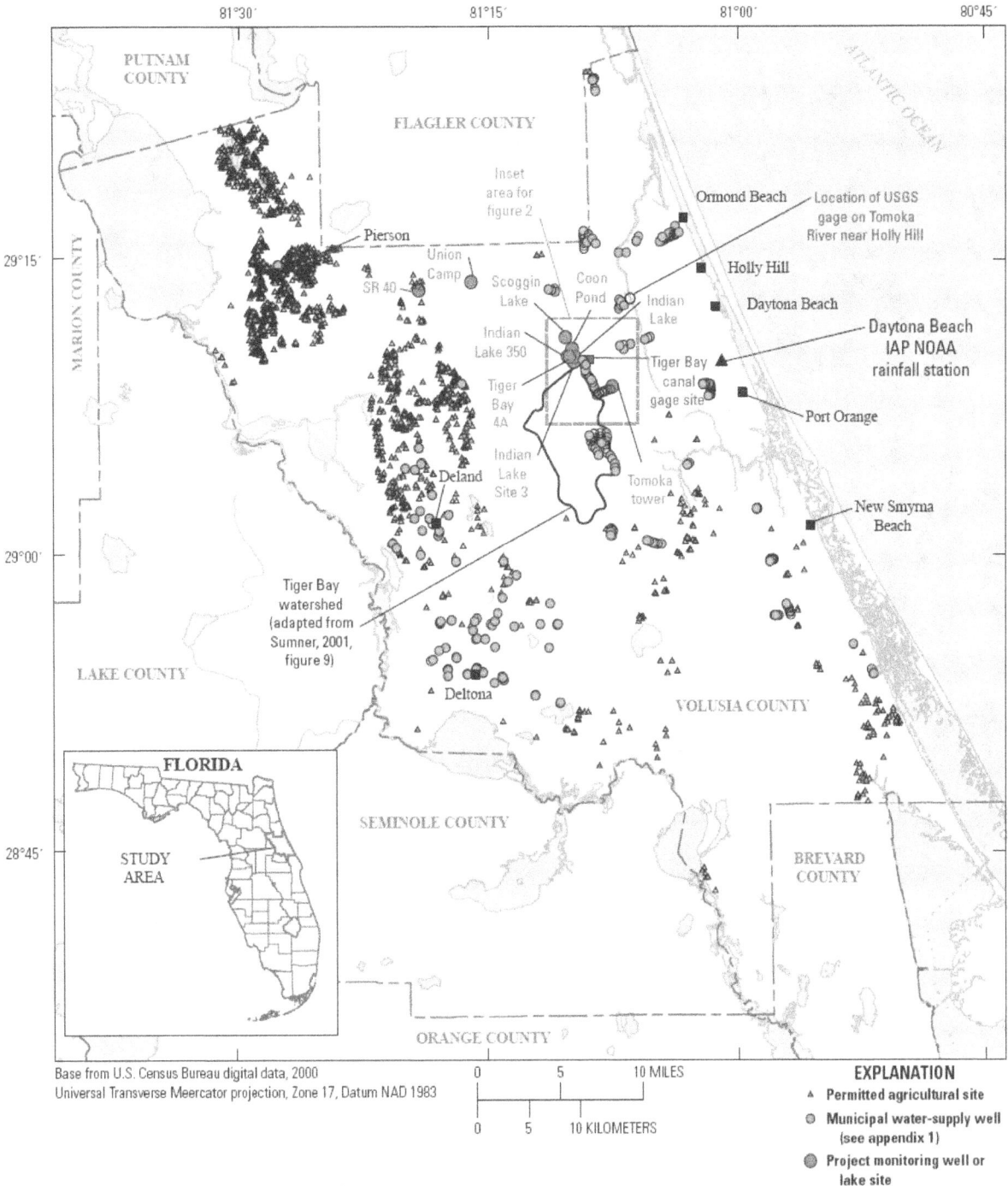

Figure 1. Location of study area, including selected monitoring well and lake sites, municipal water-supply wells, and permitted agricultural sites in Volusia County, Florida.

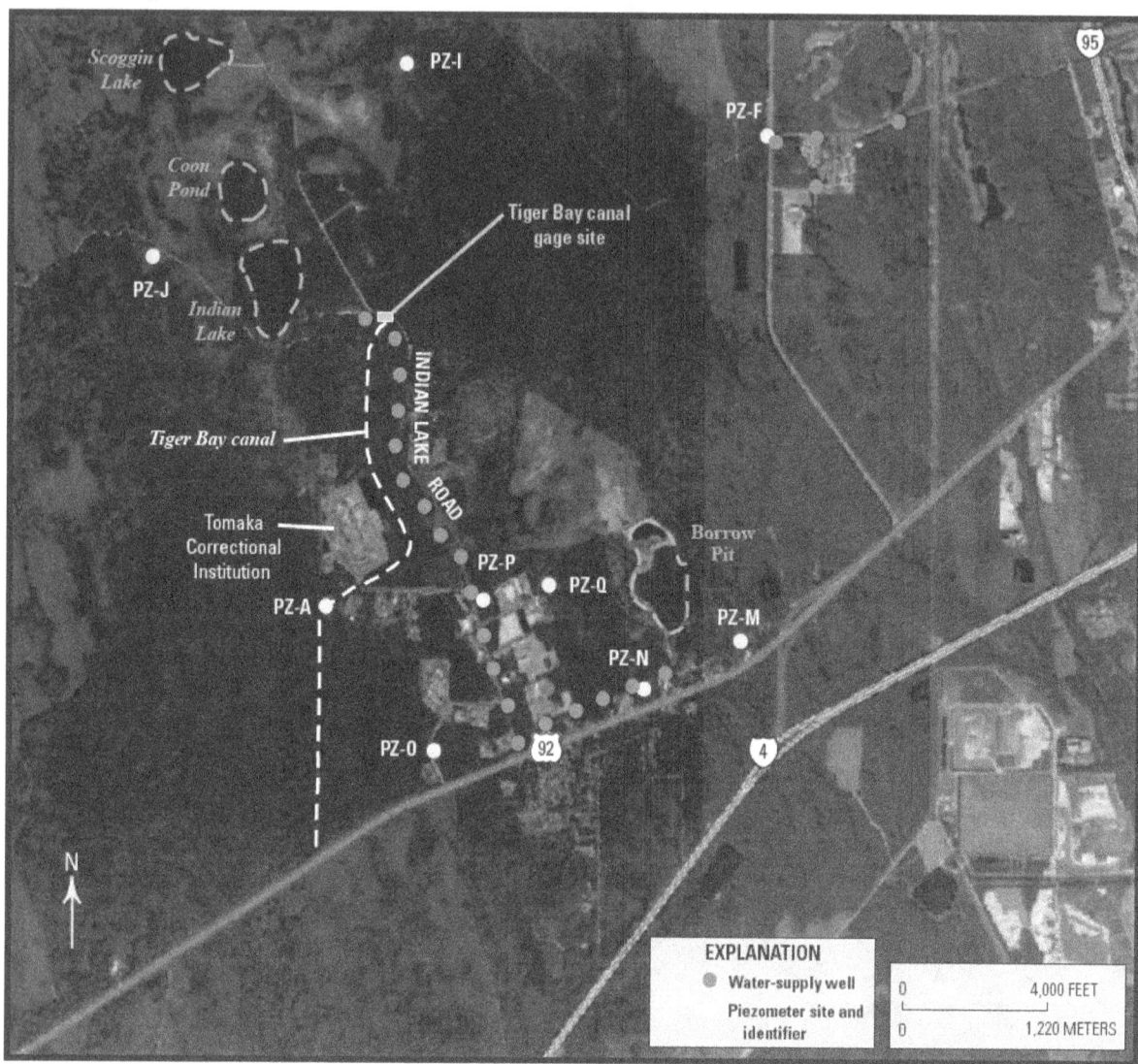

Figure 2. Locations of piezometers, municipal water-supply wells, and the Tiger Bay canal gage.

Site Descriptions and Hydrogeologic Setting

Groundwater sites include eight monitoring-well sites (Tiger Bay 4A UFA, Tomoka tower SAS, Tomoka tower UFA, SR40 SAS, SR40 UFA, Indian Lake site 3 SAS, Indian Lake 350 SAS, and Union Camp SAS) and nine SAS piezometer sites (PZ-A, PZ-F, PZ-I, PZ-J, PZ-M, PZ-N, PZ-O, PZ-P, and PZ-Q). Piezometer sites with data that satisfied the SJRWMD quality assurance/quality control screening protocols were included in these analyses. Five groundwater-monitoring wells are completed in the SAS; three are completed in the UFA. Clustered SAS and UFA monitoring wells are present at both the Tomoka tower and SR40 locations. The locations of the groundwater-monitoring and lake sites are shown in figure 1; the locations of the more-tightly grouped piezometer sites and

the Tiger Bay canal gage are shown in figure 2. Information on the water-level monitoring sites, including available periods of record, well construction specifications, and precipitation are provided in table 1. Differences in precipitation shown for the same stations in table 1. Differences in precipitation shown for the same stations in table 1 are due to differences in the periods of record (PORs) for the sites.

Most of the project sites are located within a few miles of one another and close to municipal water-supply wells (fig. 1). The Union Camp SAS and SR40 sites are about 7 to 10 miles (mi) northwest of the other sites. Although further removed from municipal withdrawals, these sites are located closer to areas of permitted agricultural acreages where UFA irrigation well withdrawals can affect water levels. Regression analyses do not take into account the effect of agricultural withdrawals,

Table 1. Water-level monitoring sites, periods of record, and related information.

[SJRWMD, St. Johns River Water Management District; UFA, Upper Floridan aquifer; SAS, surficial aquifer system; M, single monthly; W, weekly; C, continuous daily; in/mo, inches per month; Q, municipal groundwater pumpage within 12 miles of site; in/mo, inchs per month; Mgal/d, million gallons per day; np, information not provided na, not applicable. *Note* Screened intervals for piezometers (PZ) extend approximately from land surface to the bottom of the hole (James Lemine, SJRWMD, written commun., May 2011)]

Project site	SJRWMD site number	Available period of record		Frequency of measure-ment	Site type	Altitude of land surface (feet above sea level[1])	Casing length (feet)	Well depth (feet below land surface)	Average rainfall (in/mo)	Average Q (Mgal/d)	Rainfall station used in analyses
		From	To								
Tiger Bay 4A UFA	V-0086	Sep-97	Jun-07	M, C	UFA	40.40	122	222	4.4	28.4	Tomoka
Tomoka tower SAS	V-0193	Jun-03	Dec-08	C	SAS	42.76	16	25	4.4	29.9	Tomoka
Tomoka tower UFA	V-0188	Jan-95	Dec-08	C	UFA	42.77	92	150	4.5	29.0	Tomoka
SR40 SAS	V-0770	Jan-95	Dec-07	C	SAS	45.04	25	35	4.2	9.3	SR40
SR40 UFA	V-0769	Jan-95	Dec-08	C	UFA	45.05	85	440	4.2	9.4	SR40
Indian Lake site 3 SAS	V-0890	Nov-05	Dec-08	C	SAS	np	3	13	3.5	32.3	Tomoka
Indian Lake 350	V-0087	Jan-95	Dec-04	M	SAS	41 17	18	20	4.7	27.4	Tomoka
Union Camp SAS	V-0088	Jan-95	Apr-08	C	SAS	34 13	18	20	4.1	20.4	SR40
Scoggin Lake	Lake	May-05	Dec-08	W	lake	na	na	na	4.5	29.1	Tomoka
Coon Pond	Lake	Sep-01	Aug-06	W, C	lake	na	na	na	5.0	29.3	Tomoka
Indian Lake	Lake	Jul-99	Dec-08	W	lake	na	na	na	4.5	31.2	Tomoka
PZ-A	PZ-A	Jan-06	Dec-10	C	SAS	36.50	np	13	3.9	36.2	Tomoka
PZ-F	PZ-F	Jan-06	Dec-10	C	SAS	26.79	np	12	3.9	29.3	Tomoka
PZ-I	PZ-I	Jan-06	Dec-10	C	SAS	29.83	np	10	3.9	28.0	Tomoka
PZ-J	PZ-J	Jan-06	Dec-10	C	SAS	38.46	np	9	3.9	30.4	Tomoka
PZ-M	PZ-M	Jan-06	Dec-10	C	SAS	29.47	np	9	3.9	29.3	Tomoka
PZ-N	PZ-N	Jan-06	Dec-10	C	SAS	39 58	np	12	3.9	29.7	Tomoka
PZ-O	PZ-O	Jan-06	Dec-10	C	SAS	37 25	np	8	3.9	31.7	Tomoka
PZ-P	PZ-P	Jan-06	Dec-10	C	SAS	43.11	np	11	3.9	31.3	Tomoka
PZ-Q	PZ-Q	Jan-06	Dec-10	C	SAS	40 13	np	8	3.9	30.9	Tomoka

[1]Referenced to National Geodetic Datum of 1929.

which are most pronounced during the winter months when large volumes of groundwater are used to protect crops from frost and freeze.

The topography of north-central Volusia County is characterized by flat marine terraces with numerous elongated, coast-parallel wetlands and poorly drained flatlands. The wetlands are interspersed with thin sandy ridges of slightly higher topography having well-drained soils. Land-surface altitudes in the study area generally range from about 30 feet (ft) above the National Geodetic Vertical Datum of 1929 (NGVD29) in wetland areas to about 45 ft above NGVD29 along the ridges. Most of the monitoring sites are located along these ridges. The physiographic features of Volusia County are described in detail by Wyrick (1960). Much of north-central Volusia County, including the study area, lies within State-designated conservation areas where commercial development is limited. Several municipal water-supply well fields have been developed in support of nearby coastal communities.

Surface drainage is poorly developed in north-central Volusia County because little gradient exists to move water toward streams or canals, such as the Tiger Bay canal. Located near an UFA well field developed along Indian Lake Road (fig. 2), the canal drains a watershed of about 29 square miles comprised mostly of pine flatwood uplands interspersed within cypress wetlands (Sumner, 2001). Most of the surface runoff measured at the canal gage is contributed through interconnected wetlands (Riekerk and Korhnak, 2000). Water discharged through the canal is distributed across a large swamp located to the east and north of the gaged site.

Land-use modifications made within and near the watershed include a correctional facility and a 60-acre borrow pit (fig. 2). Water extracted from ponds constructed at the correctional facility between 1975 and 1981 has been used for landscape irrigation. The borrow pit, constructed just east of the watershed boundary, was used intermittently between the mid-1960s and late 2004 to provide fill material for construction projects (St. Johns River Water Management

District, written commun., 2011). Water entering the pit from overland runoff during storm events and from groundwater seepage was occasionally removed to allow for vertical excavation of the pit. It is not known if the water removed from the pit was discharged into the Tiger Bay watershed. Although land-use alterations have the potential to affect surface-water flows and groundwater levels, an assessment of such effects is beyond the scope of this study.

The principal geologic and hydrogeologic units in east-central Florida are shown in figure 3. The SAS is the uppermost water-bearing unit and consists of an unconfined sequence of Holocene to late Pliocene quartz sands with varying proportions of silt, clay, and small amounts of locally dispersed shell. The system is recharged by rainfall, and discharge occurs by evapotranspiration, by downward leakage to the UFA, and by lateral seepage to lakes.

The SAS is underlain by the intermediate confining unit (ICU), a sequence of Pliocene- to Miocene-age sands, silts, and clays that retard the vertical movement of water between the SAS and UFA. The ICU at the Tiger Bay 4A site is approximately 40-ft thick and comprised of layers of clay and shell (Rutledge, 1984). Leakance of the ICU, which is calculated by dividing the equivalent vertical hydraulic

conductivity of the unit by its thickness, influences the head differential between the SAS and UFA and controls the rate of groundwater movement between the two aquifer systems. As a result, leakance influences the potential for Upper Floridan aquifer groundwater withdrawals to affect SAS water levels; that is, the greater the leakance of the ICU, the greater the likelihood that withdrawals from the UFA will lower SAS water levels. Numerical groundwater-flow modeling indicates that the leakance in north-central Volusia County ranges from about 5×10^{-5} day^{-1} to 1×10^{-4} day^{-1} (Bush, 1978).

The ICU is underlain by the FAS, a sequence of highly permeable Eocene-age limestone and dolomitic limestone. This system consists of two major permeable zones, the UFA and the Lower Floridan aquifer (LFA), separated by a less permeable middle semiconfining unit (MSCU). The UFA provides most of the water required to meet municipal, agricultural, industrial, and commercial demands in east-central Florida. Transmissivity of the UFA in the study area, defined as the rate at which water of the prevailing kinematic viscosity is transmitted through a unit width of the aquifer under a unit hydraulic gradient, is estimated from a regional groundwater-flow model at about 13,000 feet squared per day (ft^2/d) (Bush, 1978).

SERIES		STRATIGRAPHIC UNIT	LITHOLOGY	HYDROGEOLOGIC UNIT	APPROXIMATE THICKNESS (FEET)
HOLOCENE		UNDIFFERENTIATED DEPOSITS	Alluvium, freshwater marl, peats, and muds in stream and lake bottoms. Also, some dunes and other windblown sand	SURFICIAL AQUIFER SYSTEM	0-150
PLEISTOCENE			Mostly quartz sand. Locally may contain deposits of shell and thin beds of clay		
PLIOCENE			Interbedded deposits of sand, shell fragments, and sandy clay; base may contain phosphatic clay	INTERMEDIATE CONFINING UNIT	0-500
MIOCENE		HAWTHORN GROUP	Interbedded quartz, sand, silt and clay, often phosphatic; phosphatic limestone often found at base of formation		
EOCENE	UPPER	OCALA LIMESTONE	Cream to tan, soft to hard, granular, porous, foraminiferal limestone	UPPER FLORIDAN AQUIFER	100-400
	MIDDLE	AVON PARK FORMATION	Light brown to brown, soft to hard, porous to dense, granular to chalky, fossiliferous limestone and brown, crystalline dolomite	MIDDLE CONFINING/ SEMICONFINING UNIT	100-1,000
	LOWER	OLDSMAR FORMATION	Alternating beds of light brown to white, chalky, porous, fossiliferous limestone and porous crystalline dolomite	LOWER FLORIDAN AQUIFER	700-1,500
PALEOCENE		CEDAR KEYS FORMATION	Dolomite, with considerable anhydrite and gypsum, some limestone		

Figure 3.   Geologic and hydrogeologic units in east-central Florida (modified from Murray and Halford, 1996).

The climate in central Florida is classified as semitropical humid and is characterized by warm, relatively wet summers and mild, relatively dry winters (Tibbals, 1990). Long-term (1949–2008) rainfall measured at the nearby Daytona Beach National Oceanic and Atmospheric Administration (NOAA) rainfall station averaged 49.1 inches per year (in/yr), 50 to 55 percent of which occurred between the months of June and September. Rainfall usually is unevenly distributed spatially, particularly during the summer months when it is oftentimes derived from localized thunderstorms. Summer rainfall can be substantially augmented by tropical storms or hurricanes, such as occurred in the summer of 2004 when hurricanes Charley, Frances, and Jeanne contributed to the 34 inches (in.) of rainfall measured at the Daytona Beach NOAA station in August and September of that year.

Methods of Investigation

This section describes the data-collection methods and statistical techniques applied in the study. Monthly time increments were used in regression analyses for consistency with the temporal resolution of the pumpage data provided by the SJRWMD and the Florida Department of Environmental Protection (FDEP). The monthly time increments also facilitate seasonal analyses of water-level changes. Discharge data collected at the Tiger Bay structure were analyzed across daily, monthly, and annual timescales.

Data Collection and Analyses

Data utilized for this study include: (1) mean daily UFA and SAS water levels at eight groundwater-monitoring and nine piezometer sites; (2) mean daily, weekly, and monthly lake stage at Indian Lake, Coon Pond, and Scoggin Lake; (3) mean daily discharge at gaged sites located on the Tiger Bay canal and the Tomoka River near Holly Hill, Florida (Fla.); (4) mean monthly groundwater withdrawals from municipal water-supply wells located within 12 mi of the project sites; (5) spatial coverages of permitted agricultural acreages in Volusia County; (6) precipitation at rainfall stations located at the Tomoka tower and SR40 monitoring-well sites, and at the Daytona Beach NOAA station; and (7) monthly values of PET collected by the USGS at the Tomoka tower and SR40 sites.

Continuous (daily) water levels acquired from the SJRWMD were measured with recording pressure transducers; however, periodic (weekly or monthly) measurements were made manually with either an electric tape or steel tape. Daily and weekly measurements were averaged to produce mean monthly values used in the regression analyses.

Groundwater withdrawal data were acquired from the SJRWMD and the FDEP. Because the data were provided as average monthly well field totals, individual well withdrawal rates were estimated by dividing the well field total by the number of contributing wells. Individual withdrawal rates were then summed for all the wells located within 12 mi of each project site to account for principal well fields in the northern part of the county. Up to 150 pumping wells distributed among eight utilities/municipalities were included in the analyses. A listing of individual water-supply wells located within 12 mi of the sites and associated withdrawal rates are provided in the appendixes.

Groundwater used for agricultural supplies in east-central Florida is mostly withdrawn from the UFA and can affect groundwater levels, though on a more localized basis. However, agricultural rates are not metered, making it difficult to quantify agricultural withdrawals. Rather, the relative proximities of the sites to concentrated areas of agricultural acreages (fig. 1) were used more in a qualitative sense to help explain anomalies in the regression results. Geographic Information System (GIS) software was used to identify the centroids of the permitted acreages from information provided by the SJRWMD.

Rainfall records were obtained from stations maintained by the SJRWMD at the Tomoka tower and SR40 monitoring sites. These data are considered to provide reasonably accurate measures of rainfall for the other nearby sites, notwithstanding the spatial variability in summer precipitation.

Monthly estimates of PET were calculated by the Priestley-Taylor method (Priestley and Taylor, 1972). Data required for the model were obtained from land- and satellite-based measurements of net radiation and air temperature made within 2 kilometers (1.24 mi) of the Tomoka tower and SR40 rainfall sites. These measurements were recorded in support of an ongoing USGS statewide study of PET (U.S. Geological Survey, 2009).

Four sets of regression analyses were performed on the monitoring well and lake datasets (table 2). The first set of analyses was conducted over available PORs between 1995 (the earliest year for which monthly groundwater withdrawal data were available) and 2008 for the monitoring well and lake sites, and between 2006 and 2010 for the piezometer sites. Available PORs for the monitoring well and lake sites ranged from about 3 years at Indian Lake site 3 SAS to about 14 years at Tomoka UFA and SR40 SAS/UFA. Although longer PORs were preferable, more than 10 years of record were available at 6 of the 11 monitoring well and lake sites. These PORs included wet and dry climatic extremes and averaged 4.29 inches per month (in/mo), which is similar to the long-term (1949–2008) precipitation average (4.10 in/mo) at the Daytona Beach NOAA station (fig. 1). A second set of analyses was performed on data collected between May 2000 and June 2007 at 7 of the 11 monitoring well and lake sites. This 7-year period represents the longest POR common to a majority of the sites and allows for comparison of results across common stressor conditions. A third set of analyses was conducted to account for seasonal variations in stressor conditions. Only monitoring well and lake sites having at least 10 years of available record were included in the seasonal analyses. The fourth set of analyses was conducted

Table 2.   Suite of regression analyses performed at water-level monitoring sites.

[UFA, Upper Floridan aquifer; SAS, surficial aquifer system; POR, period of record; insuff. POR, period of record was insufficient for regression analyses; insen. Q, insensitive to Q, radial analyses not performed because water-level changes were not found to be statistically correlated with pumpage cumulated within the maximum 12-mile radius; X, analyses were conducted (analyses were not conducted when no municipal groundwater withdrawals were located within a mile of the site)]

Project site	Site type	Available POR		Monthly analyses across available POR	Monthly analyses, May 2000 to June 2007	Seasonal analyses across the available POR	Drought analyses, October 2005 to June 2008	Radial analyses across the available POR
		From	To					
Tiger Bay 4A UFA	UFA	Sep-97	Jun-07	X	X	X	insuff. POR	X
Tomoka tower SAS	SAS	Jun-03	Dec-08	X	insuff. POR	insuff. POR	X	X
Tomoka tower UFA	UFA	Jan-95	Dec-08	X	X	X	X	X
SR40 SAS	SAS	Jan-95	Dec-07	X	X	X	insuff. POR	insen. to Q
SR40 UFA	UFA	Jan-95	Dec-08	X	X	X	X	insen. to Q
Indian Lake site 3 SAS	SAS	Nov-05	Dec-08	X	insuff. POR	insuff. POR	insuff. POR	X
Indian Lake 350 SAS	SAS	Jan-95	Dec-04	X	insuff. POR	X	insuff. POR	insen. to Q
Union Camp SAS	SAS	Jan-95	Apr-08	X	X	X	X	not conducted
Scoggin Lake	Lake	May-05	Dec-08	X	X	insuff. POR	X	X
Coon Pond	Lake	Sep-01	Aug-06	X	insuff. POR	insuff. POR	insuff. POR	insen. to Q
Indian Lake	Lake	Jul-99	Dec-08	X	X	insuff. POR	X	X
PZ-A	SAS	Jan-06	Dec-10	X	insuff. POR	insuff. POR	insuff. POR	X
PZ-F	SAS	Jan-06	Dec-10	X	insuff. POR	insuff. POR	insuff. POR	insen. to Q
PZ-I	SAS	Jan-06	Dec-10	X	insuff. POR	insuff. POR	insuff. POR	insen. to Q
PZ-J	SAS	Jan-06	Dec-10	X	insuff. POR	insuff. POR	insuff. POR	insen. to Q
PZ-M	SAS	Jan-06	Dec-10	X	insuff. POR	insuff. POR	insuff. POR	insen. to Q
PZ-N	SAS	Jan-06	Dec-10	X	insuff. POR	insuff. POR	insuff. POR	insen. to Q
PZ-O	SAS	Jan-06	Dec-10	X	insuff. POR	insuff. POR	insuff. POR	insen. to Q
PZ-P	SAS	Jan-06	Dec-10	X	insuff. POR	insuff. POR	insuff. POR	insen. to Q
PZ-Q	SAS	Jan-06	Dec-10	X	insuff. POR	insuff. POR	insuff. POR	insen. to Q

to examine the relations between changes in water levels and stressors during an extended period of drought from October 2005 to June 2008. Finally, regression analyses were performed to examine how radially dependent increases in cumulative groundwater withdrawals, within a maximum distance of 12 mi of each site, affected relations. This analysis compared results from regressions that accounted only for pumping wells located close to the sites with results that included the more distant wells.

A total of 24 years of discharge record (1978 to 2001) collected at the Tiger Bay canal (USGS station number 02247480) was evaluated. Procedures used to measure discharge are described by Turnipseed and Sauer (2010). The record between 1978 to 1988 is composed of measurements taken prior to development of the nearby municipal well field (completed in 1988), whereas the data collected between 1989 and 2001 are referred to as the post-development record. The well field discharged 9 to 10 million gallons per day

(Mgal/d) of groundwater between 1995 and 2010. Withdrawal rates between 1988 and 1994 were unavailable but were assumed to be similar to those between 1995 and 2010, given that the utility's service-area population changed little between the two periods.

Statistical Methods

Statistical methods and guidelines described by Helsel and Hirsch (2002) for MLR analyses were applied in this study. A commercially available statistical software package was used to conduct the regressions (Minitab Statistical Software, Inc., State College, Pennsylvania). Monthly changes in UFA and SAS water levels, calculated as the difference between the current month's mean water level and that of the previous month, were used as response variables. Twelve candidate explanatory variables were included in the regression analyses (table 3). These include (1) the three base variables of precipitation (*prec*), net available water (*prec-PET*), and municipal groundwater withdrawal (*Q*); (2) monthly changes in the three base variables (Δ*prec*, Δ*(prec-PET)* and Δ*Q*); and (3) the 2-month moving average values of the six previously listed variables to account for persistence (system memory) of water-level changes to the previous month's stressor conditions (Murray, 2010). Changes in the moving average of an explanatory variable were determined by first calculating the change in the variable from one month to the next, and then calculating the moving average of the monthly changes.

Multiple linear regression models predict the relation between a response and explanatory variable as

$$Y = \beta_0 + \beta_1 x_1 + \ldots \beta_k x_k + e \qquad (1)$$

where

Y is the response variable,

β_0 is the intercept,

β_1 is the slope coefficient for the first explanatory variable (x_1),

β_k is the slope coefficient for the kth explanatory variable (x_k), and

e is the error or remaining unexplained "noise" in the data.

The MLR tool assumes that a monotonic linear relation exists between explanatory and response variables.

Simple linear regression was used as a screening tool to reduce the number of explanatory variables used in the MLR analyses by identifying those variables best related to water-level changes. In most cases, only 4 or 5 of the 12 candidate variables were included in testing. Selected models were limited to a maximum of three explanatory variables, though most of the models included only one or two variables. All variables included in the best models had statistically significant slope coefficients (p-value less than 0.05). A p-value of less than 0.05 indicates a 5-percent probability that a detected correlation or difference is not real.

The best subsets of models were identified in MLR testing for each of "*k*" explanatory variables, with the best model selected by minimizing Mallows Cp. Mallows Cp is a test statistic designed to explain as much of the variance in the response variable as possible by including all relevant explanatory variables, while maintaining a small number of coefficients to minimize the standard error of the resulting estimates (Watts, 1995). If two best models had equal values of Cp, the one with the greater adjusted R^2 (R^2_{adj}) was selected. The R^2_{adj} quantifies the proportion of variation in the response data explained by variation in the explanatory variables while accounting for the number of explanatory variables (or equivalently, the degrees of freedom) in the model. Maximizing R^2_{adj} is equivalent to minimizing the mean square error (Helsel and Hirsch, 2002).

Table 3.   Explanatory variables used in regression analyses.

Meteorological variable	Explanation (inches)
prec	Monthly precipitation
prec$_{2ma}$	2-month moving average of precipitation
Δ*prec*	Monthly change in precipitation
Δ*prec*$_{2ma}$	2-month moving average of change in precipitation
p-pet	Monthly difference between precipitation and potential evapotranspiration
(p-pet)$_{2ma}$	2-month moving average of the difference between precipitation and potential evapotranspiration
Δ*(p-pet)*	Monthly change in the difference between precipitation and potential evapotranspiration
Δ*(p-pet)*$_{2ma}$	2-month moving average of the change in the difference between precipitation and potential evapotranspiration

Anthropogenic variable	Explanation (million gallons per day)
Q	Cumulative monthly groundwater pumpage from municipal supply wells located within 12 miles of the site
Q$_{2ma}$	2-month moving average of groundwater pumpage located within 12 miles of the site
Δ*Q*	Monthly change in groundwater pumpage located within 12 miles of the site
Δ*Q*$_{2ma}$	2-month moving average of change in groundwater pumpage located within 12 miles of the site

Models containing a variable with a variance inflation factor (VIF) exceeding 2.0 were considered to have unacceptably high levels of multicollinearity and were excluded. Multicollinearity is the condition where at least one explanatory variable is closely related to one or more other explanatory variables (Helsel and Hirsch, 2002). The VIF is an index that measures how much the variance of a coefficient is increased because of multicollinearity. The value of 2.0 used in these regressions was arbitrarily selected to provide a more rigorous benchmark for identifying unacceptable levels of multicollinearity (Ken Eng, U.S. Geological Survey, oral commun., 2010) than the value of 10 recommended by Helsel and Hirsch (2002).

Models with explanatory variables having slope coefficients that were hydrologically untenable were excluded, even though such models may have provided lower Cp and/or higher R^2_{adj} values. In early testing, for example, PET was found to be directly (and not inversely) related to changes in water levels when included as a single variable. Relations such as these are usually attributable to multicollinearity between PET and one of the other variables included in the best model, such as precipitation (Dennis Helsel, Practical Stats, Inc., written commun., 2009). PET and precipitation are greatest in the warm summer months, yet the two variables work in opposite directions in terms of their effects on water levels. Accordingly, PET is not listed on table 3 as a stand-alone variable but was included with precipitation as a lumped parameter (*prec–PET*) to provide a gross estimate of the amount of water available to recharge the SAS (Murray, 2010).

The Durbin-Watson statistic D_L (Durbin and Watson, 1951) was used to determine if the time series of regression residuals indicated that changes in monthly water levels were serially correlated. Regression analyses using serially correlated data will yield erroneous values of R^2_{adj} and the standard error, and may result in concluding that a statistically significant relation exists between the response and explanatory variables when one does not. Values of D_L calculated by the Minitab software for the given number of observations, predictor variables in the regression equation, and significance level (0.05) were compared with threshold values tabulated by Montgomery and Peck (1982, table A.6, p. 478) to determine if residuals were positively or negatively correlated. A D_L value equal to 2.0 indicates no serial correlation. For D_L values of less than 2.0, residuals were considered to be positively correlated if D_L was less than the lower threshold value tabulated in table A.6 of Montgomery and Peck (1982). For D_L values of greater than 2.0, residuals were considered to be negatively correlated if $(4 - D_L)$ was less than the lower tabulated threshold value.

Regression residuals were evaluated for normality and were plotted against predicted values to assess linearity and scatter. The dependent variable was log-transformed in cases where assumptions were violated or when such transformations improved R^2_{adj} values. A Kolmogorov test (Conover, 1999) was applied to test if monthly residuals were normally distributed about respective means. The test calculates a p-value to determine whether or not the null hypothesis (that the residuals are normally distributed) can be accepted. P-values of less than 0.05 indicate that the null hypothesis can be rejected, whereas p-values equal to or greater than 0.05 indicate that the residuals are normally distributed. Partial residual plots were examined for linearity and scatter to determine if explanatory variables required log transformation.

The relative influence of explanatory variables on water-level changes was assessed by comparing coefficient p-values. In a model having both climatic and anthropogenic variables, for example, the variable with the lower coefficient p-value explained more of the variance in water-level changes, and was thus considered to be more highly correlated with the response variable. Based on comparison of p-values, an empirical constant, hereafter called the stressor influence value (SIV), was assigned to each site as a convenient means for comparing results from one site to the next, and from one set of analyses to the next (Murray, 2010). The SIVs range from "1" for sites having water-level changes correlated solely

with precipitation to "5" for sites having changes correlated solely with groundwater withdrawals. In cases where the two variables had p-values of less than 0.001, which is the lower limit reported by the Minitab software package, water-level changes were considered to be highly correlated with both variables and assigned an SIV of "3." In cases where precipitation is more highly correlated with water-level changes than groundwater withdrawals, a SIV of "2" is indicated, whereas a SIV of "4" is indicated where withdrawals are more highly correlated with water-level changes than precipitation.

Streamflow data collected at the Tiger Bay canal site were analyzed using several methods. Flow-duration curves (Searcy, 1959) were developed and contrasted for pre- and post- well-field development periods. The shapes and slopes of flow-duration curves, particularly during low-flow regimes, can identify changes in the amount of groundwater discharging into the canal. The median number of zero-flow days was contrasted between pre- and post- well-field development periods using a Mann-Whitney test (Helsel and Hirsch, 2002). The Mann-Whitney test is a nonparametric (ranked-based) method that is more robust than the parametric two-sample t-test for nonnormally distributed data. The test is robust because it is not highly influenced by extreme values (outliers) in the data. The null hypothesis for the Mann-Whitney test is that the median number of zero-flow days was similar before and after well-field development. Kendall's tau (Helsel and Hirsch, 2002) was used to test for temporal trends in the number of days having zero flow and for precipitation between 1978 and 2001. The Kendall tau test is a nonparametric procedure that measures the strength of a monotonic relation, whether linear or nonlinear, between the response and explanatory variables. Typically, the null hypothesis for the Kendall tau test is that a monotonic relation does not exist. A probability level of 5 percent was used in all statistical tests as the criterion for significance. If the probability level was less than 5 percent, then the null hypothesis was rejected and the differences were statistically significant. Conversely, if the probability level was at least 5 percent, then the null hypothesis was accepted and the differences were not statistically significant.

A double-mass curve was constructed using discharges measured at the Tiger Bay and Tomoka River sites. Double-mass curves are commonly constructed to compare streamflow regimes in nearby watersheds. The assumption is that streamflows in nearby watersheds will co-vary, because they are influenced by similar climatic and hydrologic conditions. These analyses are useful for identifying watershed-level changes in stream discharge, such as increases or decreases in groundwater contributions to base flow, the appearance of natural or manmade dams, and other watershed-level phenomena. In this report, double-mass curves are used to identify changes in the streamflow relation between the Tiger Bay and Tomoka River sites, which may be attributed to groundwater withdrawal or to some other change in hydrologic conditions in either of the two watersheds. Techniques used in these analyses are described by Searcy and Hardison (1960).

Hydrologic Conditions during the Study Period

Hydrologic and groundwater withdrawal conditions that existed at the study sites for the selected periods of record are presented in the following sections. Descriptions are provided for water levels, discharge in the Tiger Bay canal, rainfall, potential evapotranspiration, and municipal groundwater withdrawals.

Water Levels

Mean monthly water levels and change in water levels are plotted across available PORs for the 20 water-level monitoring sites shown in figure 4. The range of monthly water-level fluctuations is less than 10 ft at all sites. The most prominent characteristic of each hydrograph is the abrupt water-level decline during the October 2005 to June 2008 drought. Excluding outliers associated with unusually high rainfall events and droughts, the change in mean monthly water levels typically ranged between -2 and 2 ft. At the Tomoka tower and SR40 cluster sites, water levels in the SAS are greater than those in the UFA, indicative of UFA recharge conditions. Although water levels in the two aquifers closely mirror each other, head differences of about 10 to 15 ft indicate a degree of UFA confinement, consistent with the previously referenced ICU leakance values.

The PORs and number of monthly observations vary from one site to the next (from 38 observations at Indian Lake site 3 SAS to 168 observations at Tomoka tower UFA and SR40 UFA) (table 4), so direct comparison of statistics between sites should be made with caution. However, mean monthly water-level changes were negative at most sites, likely due to the magnitudes and frequency of monthly declines associated with the October 2005 to June 2008 drought. In the eight monitoring well and lake sites having greater than 100 observations, the average monthly water-level change is -0.025 ft, with an average standard deviation of 0.91 ft. PORs for the SAS and UFA at the SR40 cluster sites are comparable, and have average monthly water-level changes of -0.026 and -0.017 ft, respectively, with standard deviations of 0.77 and 0.72 ft, respectively. By comparison, water-level declines measured in the piezometers (average of -0.071 ft) from 2006 to 2010 are considerably greater than those measured at the monitoring-well sites and lakes. This difference can be attributed to the greater percentage of the piezometer POR being characterized by drought.

Discharge in Tiger Bay Canal

Mean daily discharge measured at the Tiger Bay canal between January 1978 and September 2002 averaged 17.4 cubic feet per second (ft^3/s) and varied from 0 ft^3/s to greater than 300 ft^3/s (fig. 5). Annually, median daily discharge ranged from 0 ft^3/d in numerous years to 23 ft^3/d in 1984 (table 5). Little baseflow contributed water to this site; rather, the large variability of measured canal flow, and the frequent peaks and recessions, are more indicative of contributions by surface runoff which occurred during wetter periods of record. Although base-flow contributions may be relatively small, these contributions are likely significant, particularly with regard to the number of zero-flow days measured at the site. Days of zero flow typically occur during the drier winter and spring seasons, and during periods of drought. On average, 144 days of zero flow per year were observed at the site between 1978 and 2001, ranging from 0 days in 1982 through 1984 to 285 days in 2000. Annual precipitation measured at the Daytona Beach NOAA station between 1982 and 1984 averaged 57 in/yr, compared to the long-term (1949 to 2008) average of 49 in/yr. Precipitation in 2000 totaled 40 in.

Rainfall and Potential Evapotranspiration

The monthly distribution of precipitation at the Tomoka tower site between 1995 and 2010 averaged 54.2 in/yr and ranged from 28.4 in 2006 to 68.1 in 2001 (fig. 6). A simple linear regression of precipitation was conducted that compared the Tomoka tower and Daytona Beach NOAA sites between March 1999 and December 2008 to estimated precipitation from January 1995 to February 1999 at the former site prior to its installation. The high coefficient of determination resulting from this analysis ($R^2 = 0.92$) supports this approach for estimating the missing record. The long-term record at the Daytona Beach NOAA station (1949 to 2008) was also used to construct a cumulative rainfall departure curve to identify a period of drought examined in this study.

PET depicts a consistent seasonal pattern with rates greatest between June and September, and least between December and March (fig. 6). Largest negative differences between precipitation and PET typically occur in late spring and in drier-than-normal summer months, whereas greatest positive differences occur in wetter-than-normal winter months. Any difference between precipitation and PET was considered to be an estimate of the minimum amount of water available to recharge the SAS, because actual evapotranspiration rates may be less than those estimated for this study. This was particularly true where the water table was several feet below land surface, a common occurrence during drier months of the year. Theoretically derived estimates, however, are probably reasonable estimates of actual evapotranspiration rates at the three MFL lakes, where losses are limited more by meteorological conditions (such as incoming solar radiation and wind conditions) than by surface-water supply.

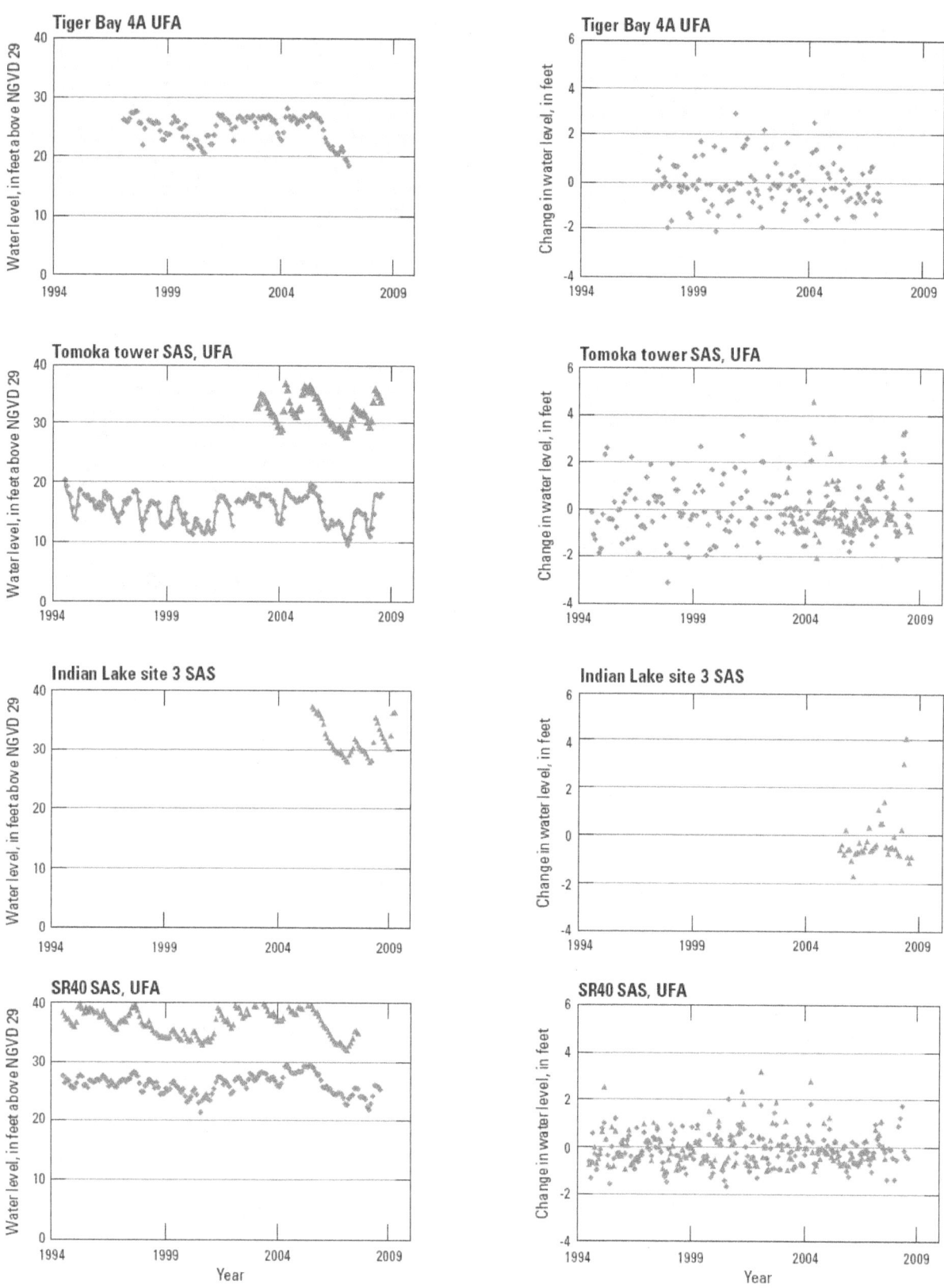

Figure 4. Monthly water levels and water-level changes across available periods of record at project sites. Red symbols represent surficial aquifer (SAS) water levels; blue symbols represent Upper Floridan aquifer (UFA) water levels.

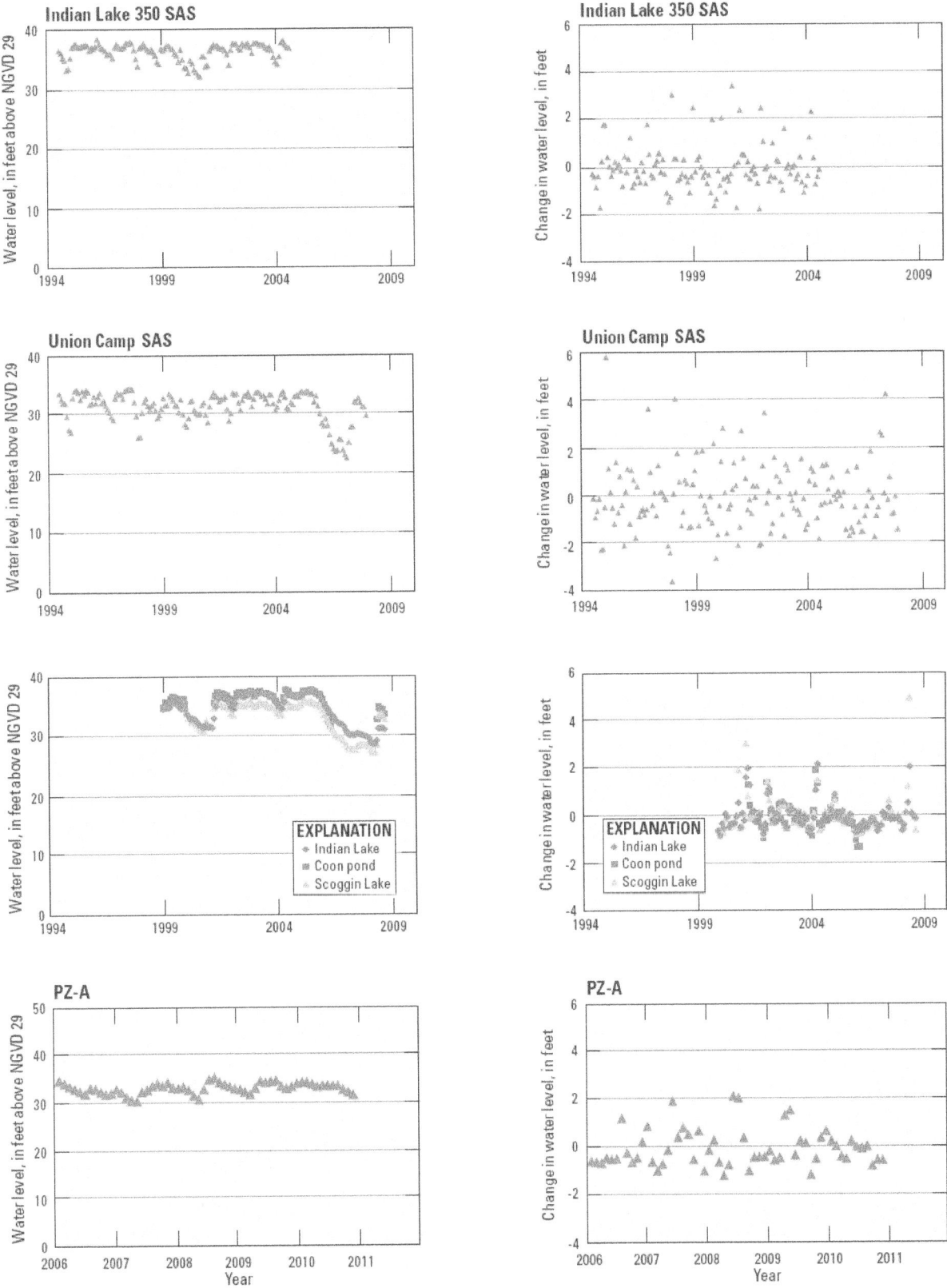

Figure 4. Monthly water levels and water-level changes across available periods of record at project sites. Red symbols represent surficial aquifer (SAS) water levels; blue symbols represent Upper Floridan aquifer (UFA) water levels.—Continued

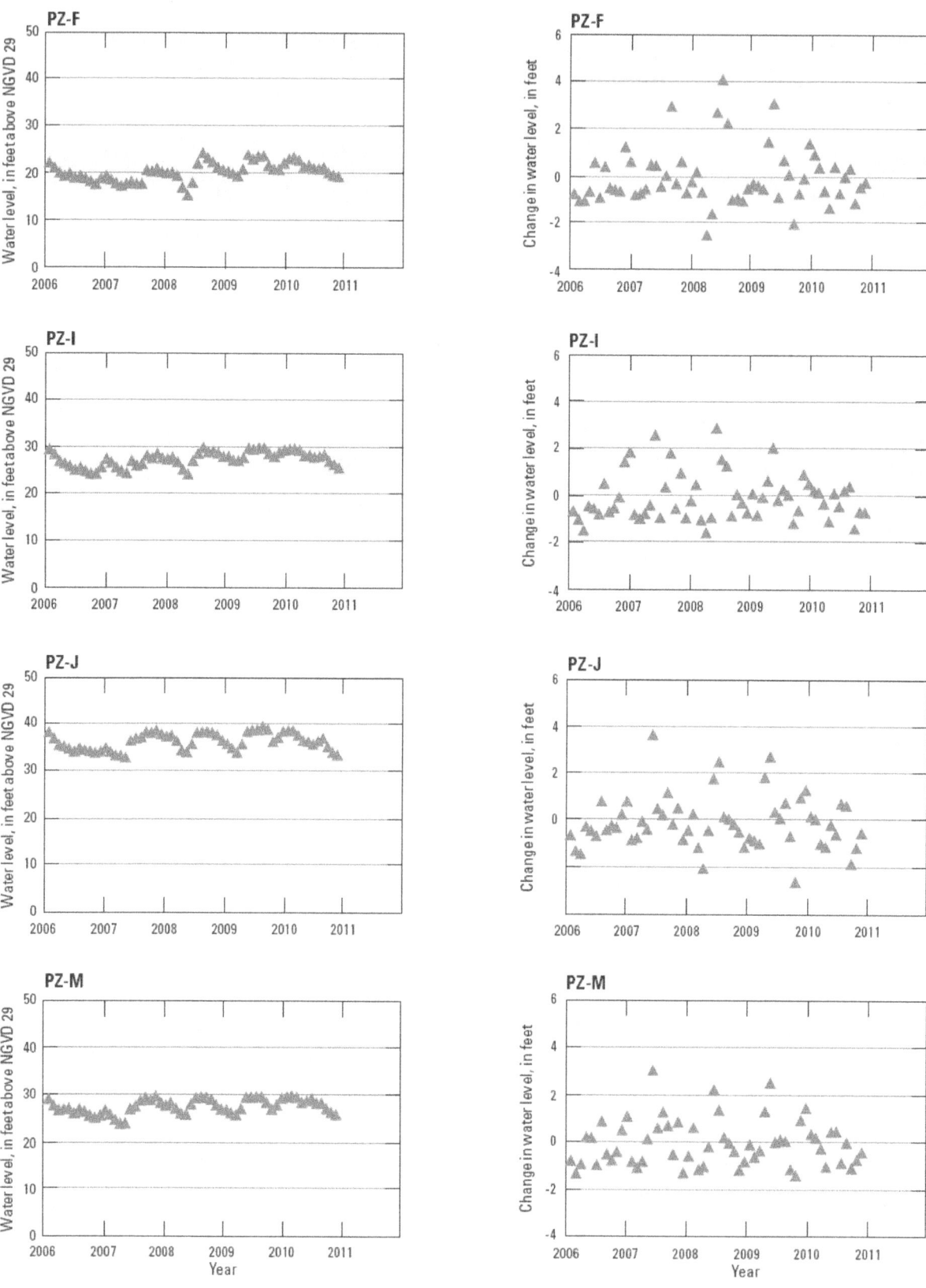

Figure 4. Monthly water levels and water-level changes across available periods of record at project sites. Red symbols represent surficial aquifer (SAS) water levels; blue symbols represent Upper Floridan aquifer (UFA) water levels.—Continued

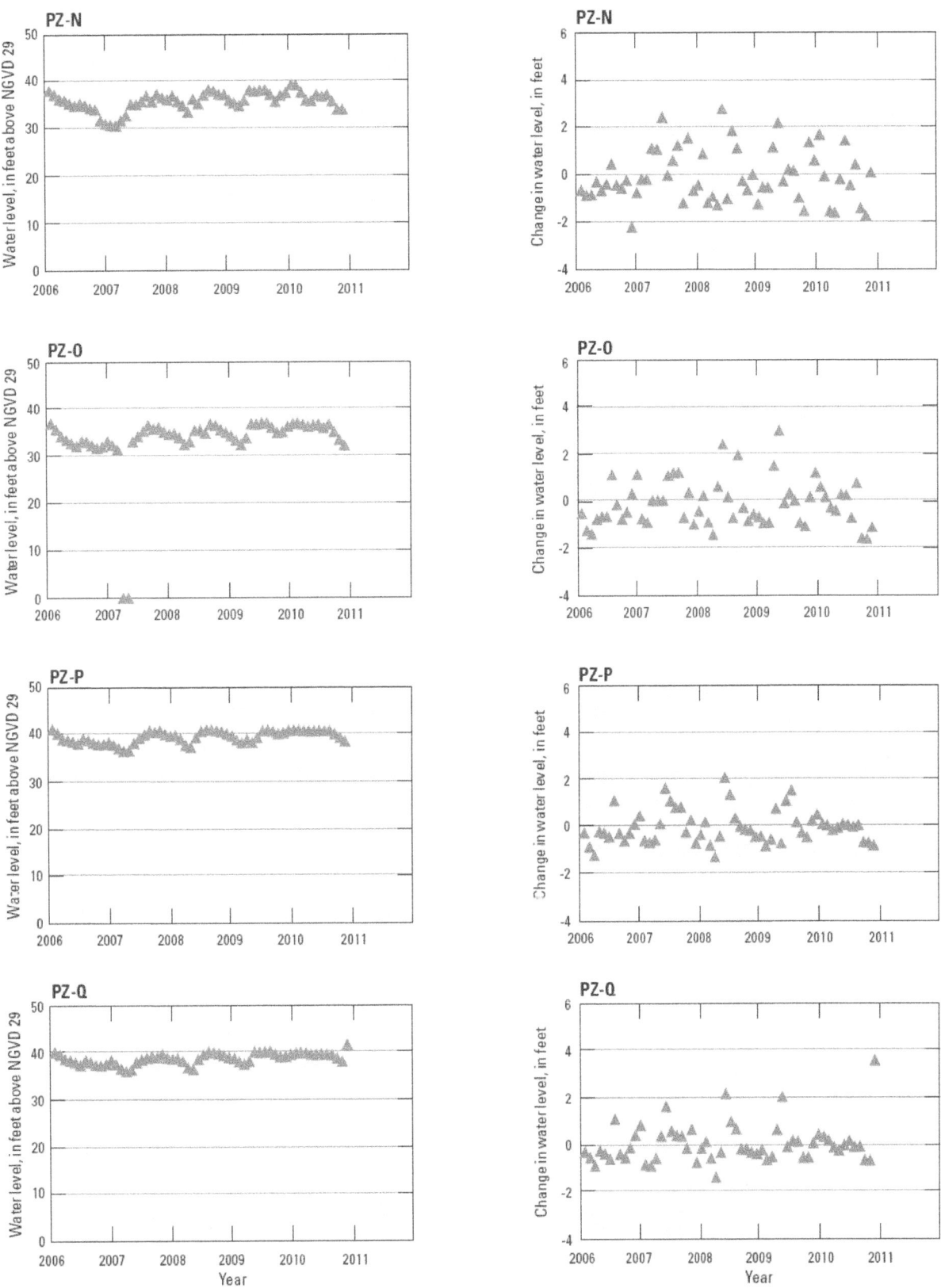

Figure 4.   Monthly water levels and water-level changes across available periods of record at project sites. Red symbols represent surficial aquifer (SAS) water levels; blue symbols represent Upper Floridan aquifer (UFA) water levels.—Continued

Table 4. Descriptive statistics for monthly changes in water levels at project sites.

[UFA, Upper Floridan aquifer; SAS, surficial aquifer system; Q, monthly groundwater pumpage from municipal supply wells located within 12 miles of the site]

Project site	Aquifer	Period of record		Number of observa-tions	Mean (feet)	Standard deviation (feet)	Minimum value (feet)	First quartile Q1 (feet)	Median value (feet)	Third quartile Q3 (feet)	Maximum value (feet)	Q3–Q1 (feet)
		From	To									
Monitoring well and lake sites												
Tiger Bay 4A UFA	UFA	Sep-97	Jun-07	118	-0.065	0.96	-2.04	-0.70	-0.16	0.43	2.95	1.13
Tomoka tower SAS	SAS	Jun-03	Dec-08	67	0.014	1.17	-2.02	-0.67	-0.36	0.41	4.59	1.08
Tomoka tower UFA	UFA	Jan-95	Dec-08	168	-0.014	1.15	-3.08	-0.70	-0.17	0.60	3.33	1.30
SR40 SAS	SAS	Jan-95	Dec-07	156	-0.026	0.77	-1.03	-0.58	-0.28	0.30	3.26	0.88
SR40 UFA	UFA	Jan-95	Dec-08	168	-0.017	0.72	-1.61	-0.50	-0.08	0.41	2.09	0.91
Indian Lake site 3 SAS	SAS	Nov-05	Dec-08	38	-0.132	1.08	-1.64	-0.69	-0.48	0.09	4.14	0.78
Indian Lake 350 SAS	SAS	Jan-95	Dec-04	120	0.000	0.96	-1.77	-0.55	-0.20	0.32	3.42	0.87
Union Camp SAS	SAS	Dec-95	Apr-08	160	-0.024	1.39	-3.59	-0.86	-0.13	0.73	5.84	1.59
Scoggin Lake	Lake	May-00	Dec-08	104	-0.023	0.76	-0.84	-0.44	-0.12	0.11	4.95	0.55
Coon Pond	Lake	Sep-01	Aug-06	60	-0.063	0.60	-1.34	-0.31	-0.13	0.13	1.88	0.44
Indian Lake	Lake	Jul-99	Dec-08	114	-0.031	0.55	-0.83	-0.35	-0.15	0.10	2.17	0.45
Average for the 8 sites having greater than 100 observations ——					-0.025	0.91						
Piezometer sites (all in surficial aquifer system)												
PZ-A	SAS	Jan-06	Dec-10	60	-0.068	0.77	-1.19	-0.58	-0.38	0.29	2.10	0.87
PZ-F	SAS	Jan-06	Dec-10	60	-0.073	1.22	-2.51	-0.78	-0.44	0.45	4.08	1.23
PZ-I	SAS	Jan-06	Dec-10	60	-0.081	0.99	-1.60	-0.81	-0.34	0.37	2.86	1.18
PZ-J	SAS	Jan-06	Dec-10	60	-0.097	1.11	-2.64	-0.76	-0.26	0.45	3.62	1.21
PZ-M	SAS	Jan-06	Dec-10	60	-0.073	0.98	-1.44	-0.85	-0.19	0.47	3.00	1.32
PZ-N	SAS	Jan-06	Dec-10	60	-0.083	1.10	-2.23	-0.85	-0.28	0.59	2.76	1.44
PZ-O	SAS	Jan-06	Dec-10	60	-0.130	0.99	-1.65	-0.83	-0.44	0.32	2.95	1.15
PZ-P	SAS	Jan-06	Dec-10	60	-0.052	0.70	-1.33	-0.56	-0.20	0.21	2.04	0.77
PZ-Q	SAS	Jan-06	Dec-10	60	0.015	0.82	-1.40	-0.56	-0.17	0.34	3.55	0.90
Average for piezometer sites ——					-0.071	0.96						

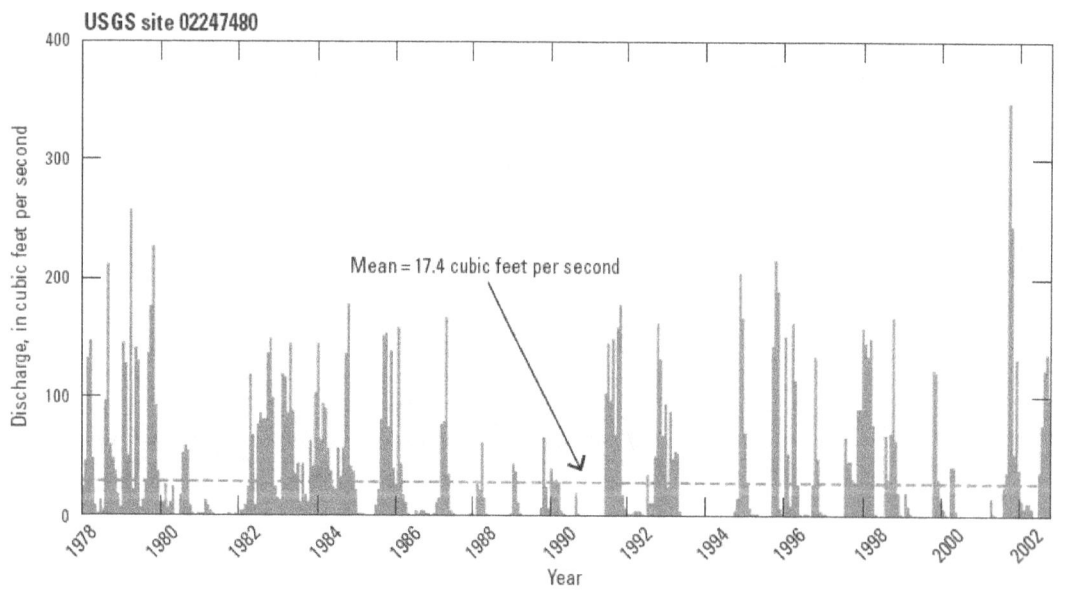

Figure 5. Daily discharge at Tiger Bay canal, January 1978–September 2002.

Table 5. Number of days of zero discharge and precipitation at Tiger Bay canal, 1978–2002.

[Annual precipitation was taken from the Daytona Beach National Oceanic and Atmospheric Administration rainfall station. ft³/s, cubic feet per second]

Year	Number of days of zero discharge	Median daily discharge (ft³/s)	Precipitation (inches)
1978	51	11.00	53.9
1979	7	20.00	69.0
1980	100	2.00	37.4
1981	226	0.00	39.7
1982	0	18.00	50.2
1983	0	22.00	74.0
1984	0	23.00	46.7
1985	126	4.30	45.4
1986	125	0.67	48.0
1987	183	0.00	45.7
1988	240	0.00	40.9
1989	205	0.00	44.7
1990	227	0.00	36.1
1991	156	1.60	67.2
1992	91	2.20	46.4
1993	245	0.00	35.7
1994	272	0.00	66.6
1995	133	0.61	54.4
1996	91	1.90	60.5
1997	175	0.13	54.7
1998	91	7.00	40.5
1999	236	0.00	46.4
2000	285	0.00	40.2
2001	190	0.00	58.3
[1]2002	76	5.50	45.5

[1]As of September 30, 2002.

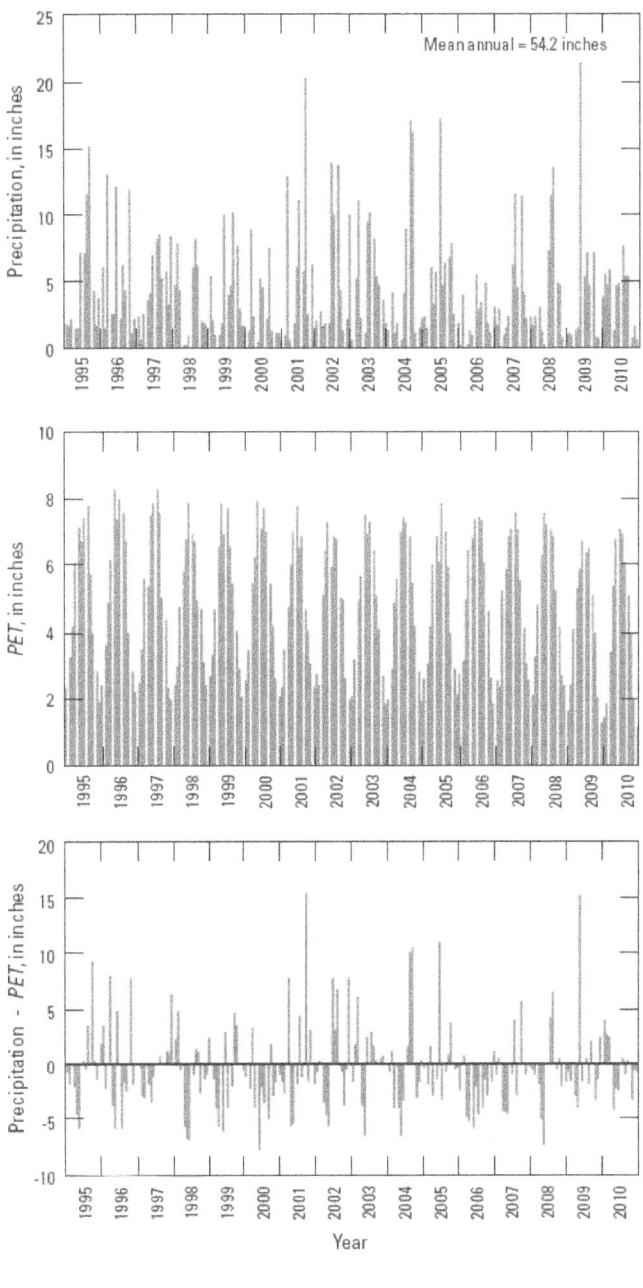

Figure 6. Monthly precipitation, potential evapotranspiration, and difference between precipitation and potential evapotranspiration at the Tomoka rainfall station, 1995–2010.

Groundwater Withdrawals

Groundwater-withdrawal rates aggregated with increasing radial distances from the monitoring well, lake, and piezometer sites are plotted in figure 7. Most sites depict similar patterns, given the close proximities to one another. The SR40 and Union Camp SAS monitoring-well sites, however, are located northwest of the main cluster and are further removed from municipal well fields. Average monthly pumping rates summed within 12 mi of the project sites vary from 9.4 Mgal/d at SR40 to 32.2 Mgal/d at Indian Lake site 3 SAS.

Variations in monthly groundwater-withdrawal rates near the Tomoka tower site (fig. 8) exhibit patterns considered representative of the other sites having similar PORs. A long-term change in withdrawals rates is not evident, but short-term seasonal fluctuations are apparent. Largest withdrawals typically occur between April and June, whereas smallest withdrawals occur between October and December. Groundwater withdrawals aggregated within 12 mi of the Tomoka tower site averaged about 29 Mgal/d between 1995 and 2008.

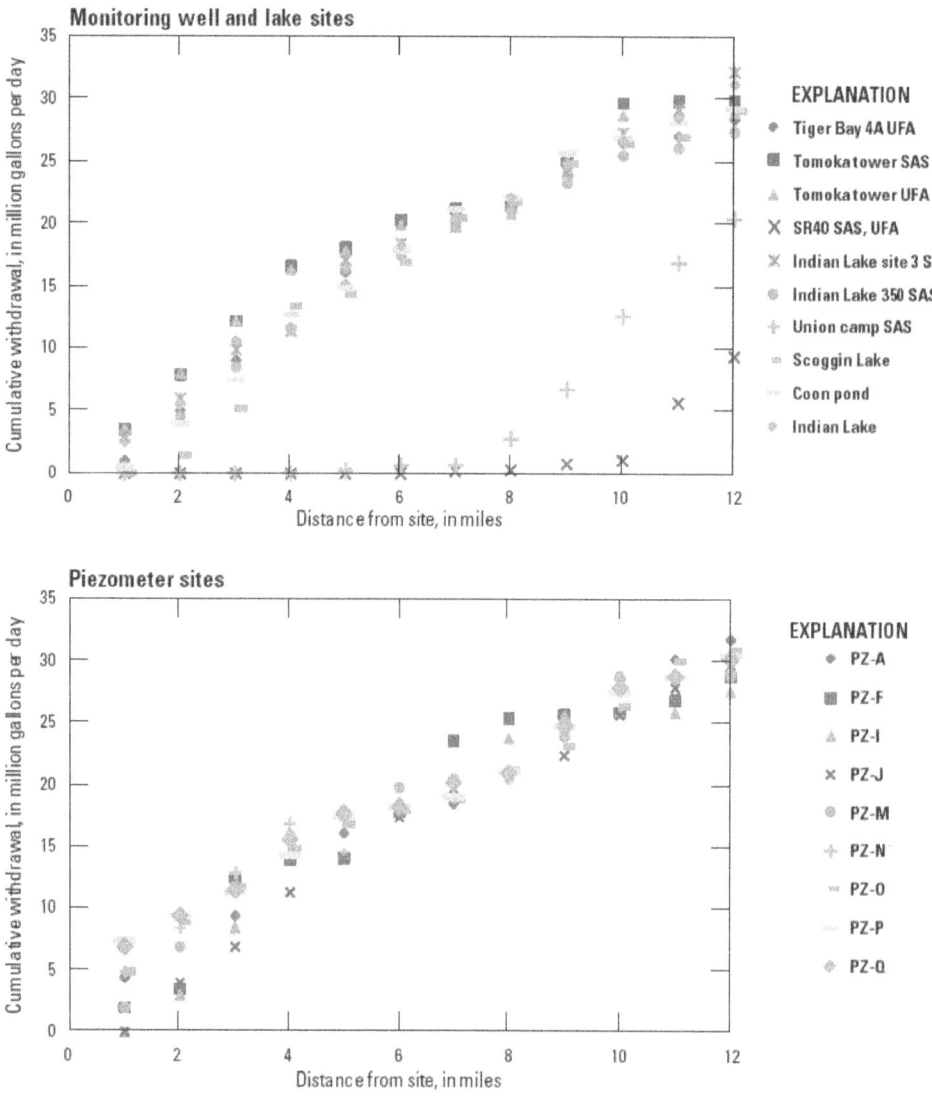

Figure 7. Cumulative municipal groundwater withdrawals with distance from monitoring well, lake, and piezometer sites.

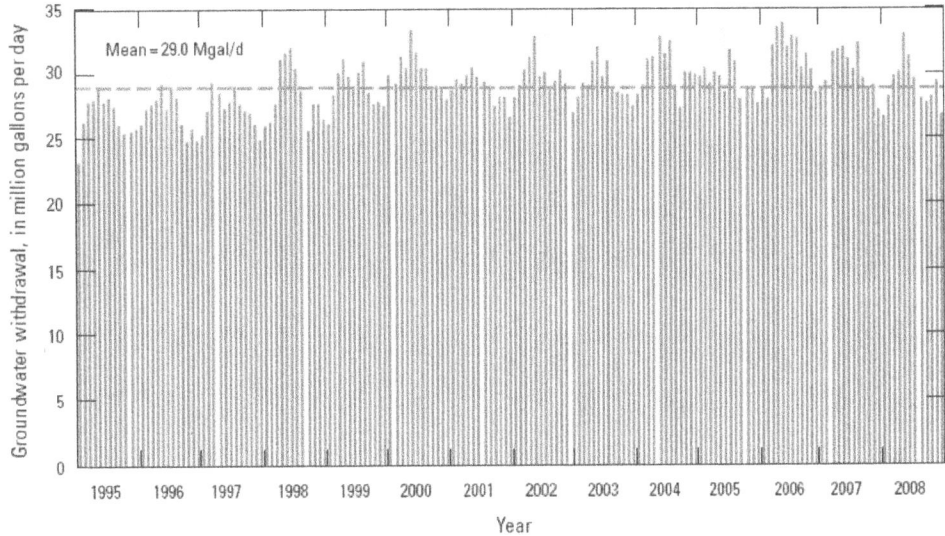

Figure 8.   Groundwater withdrawals within 12 miles of the Tomoka tower site, 1995–2008.

Relations between Precipitation, Groundwater Withdrawals, and Changes in Hydrologic Conditions

Regression results are summarized in a series of tables that document selected model equations, explanatory variables included in the equations, coefficient p-values for the explanatory variables, and regression statistics (R^2_{adj}, VIF, and D_L). The coefficient p-value indicates whether a given explanatory variable is statistically correlated with the response variable with sufficient strength to include in the equation (p-values of less than 0.05). Explanatory variables with p-values greater than 5 percent were not considered statistically important to the regression and were not included in the final regression equation.

Analyses of Water-Level Changes across Available Periods of Record

Regression models developed for the 20 water-level monitoring sites include one to three statistically significant explanatory variables that reflect varying influences of precipitation and groundwater withdrawals on changes in water levels (table 6a). Explanatory variables account for greater than 60 percent of the variance in water-level changes at 11 of the 20 sites. Adjusted R^2 (R^2_{adj}) ranged from 33 percent at PZ-N to 81 percent at Tomoka tower SAS. All VIF values are less than 2.0, indicating that multicollinearity among explanatory variables is not statistically significant. Similarly, calculated D_L values are all below associated threshold values reported in table A.6 of Montgomery and Peck (1982), indicating no

statistical evidence exists that the residuals are serially correlated. Finally, the slope coefficients for explanatory variables are reasonable; that is, changes in water levels are directly related to precipitation and inversely related to groundwater withdrawal.

The 2-month moving averages of precipitation ($prec_{2ma}$) and change in precipitation ($\Delta prec_{2ma}$) are the climatic variables most frequently included in the equations, whereas the 2-month moving averages of groundwater withdrawal (Q_{2ma}) and change in withdrawal (ΔQ_{2ma}) are the most common anthropogenic variables (table 6b). These results reflect the need to account not only for the effects of current monthly stressor conditions, but also for those of the previous month.

Changes in water levels were statistically correlated with precipitation at each of the eight groundwater-monitoring sites and with groundwater withdrawals at five of the eight monitoring sites (table 6b). Based on comparison of coefficient p-values, water-level changes at the two UFA sites closest to areas of concentrated groundwater withdrawals (Tiger Bay 4A UFA and Tomoka tower UFA) were highly correlated with both precipitation and withdrawal (SIV = 3), whereas changes in SAS water levels were more highly correlated with precipitation than with withdrawals (SIV = 2) at Tomoka tower SAS, Indian Lake site 3 SAS, and Union Camp SAS, or were correlated solely with precipitation (SIV = 1) at SR40 SAS and Indian Lake site 350 SAS. Given that groundwater is extracted from the UFA and not from the SAS, it is not surprising that changes in water levels at Tiger Bay 4A UFA and Tomoka tower UFA were more affected by withdrawals than were changes in SAS water levels. Similarly, it is reasonable to expect that changes measured in both aquifers at both SR40 sites, which are further removed from municipal well fields, would be less affected (or altogether unaffected) by withdrawals.

Table 6a. Regression equations chosen to model the change in water levels at 20 groundwater and lake monitoring sites in the study area.

[UFA, Upper Floridan aquifer; SAS, surficial aquifer system; GW, groundwater monitoring site; SW, surface-water monitoring site; VIF, variance inflation factor; D_L, Durbin statistic; R^2_{adj}, adjusted coefficient of determination; $prec$, monthly precipitation, in inches; $prec_{2ma}$, 2-month moving average of $prec$, in inches; $\Delta prec_{2ma}$, 2-month moving average of change in $prec$, in inches; pet, monthly potential evapotranspiration, in inches; $(p-pet)_{2ma}$, 2-month moving average of the difference between $prec$ and pet, in inches; $\Delta(p-pet)_{2ma}$, 2-month moving average of change in $(p-pet)$, in inches; Q_{2ma}, 2-month moving average of pumpage, in million gallons per day; ΔQ, monthly change in pumpage, in million gallons per day; ΔQ_{2ma}, 2-month moving average of change in pumpage, in million gallons per day]

Project site	Site type	Period of record From	Period of record To	Best regressed equation	VIF	D_L	R^2_{adj}
Tiger Bay 4A UFA	GW	Sep-97	Jun-07	$\Delta UFA = -2.63 + 0.121*\Delta prec_{2ma} + 1.17*\ln((p-pet)_{2ma}+10) - 0.258*\Delta Q$	1.27	2.09	0.64
Tokoma tower SAS	GW	Jun-03	Dec-08	$\Delta SAS = -0.12 + 0.259*prec_{2ma} + 0.952*\ln(\Delta prec_{2ma}+10) - 0.106*Q_{2ma}$	1.13	1.66	0.81
Tokoma tower UFA	GW	Jan-95	Dec-08	$\Delta UFA = \exp(2.20 + 0.0764*\ln(prec_{2ma}) - 0.0408*\Delta Q_{2ma}) - 10$	1.44	2.13	0.60
SR40 SAS	GW	Jan-95	Dec-07	$\Delta SAS = -0.772 + 0.179*prec_{2ma} + 0.0750*\Delta prec_{2ma}$	1.24	2.09	0.61
SR40 UFA	GW	Jan-95	Dec-08	$\Delta UFA = -0.727 + 0.171*prec_{2ma}$	1.00	2.03	0.45
Indian Lake site 3 SAS	GW	Nov-05	Dec-08	$\Delta SAS = \exp(2.57 + 0.0256*prec_{2ma} - 0.0117*Q_{2ma}) - 10$	1.01	1.87	0.62
Indian Lake site 350 SAS	GW	Jan-95	Dec-04	$\Delta SAS = \exp(2.25 + 0.0429*\ln(prec) + 0.0083*\Delta prec_{2ma}) - 10$	1.61	2.32	0.45
Union Camp SAS	GW	Jan-95	Apr-08	$\Delta SAS = \exp(1.95 + 0.0174*\Delta prec_{2ma} + 0.161*\ln((p-pet)_{2ma} + 10) - 0.0476*\Delta Q_{2ma}) - 10$	1.26	1.94	0.43
PZ-A	GW	Jan-06	Dec-10	$\Delta SAS = -1.21 + 0.161*prec_{2ma} + 0.949*\ln(\Delta prec_{2ma} + 10) - 0.050*Q$	1.11	1.97	0.66
PZ-F	GW	Jan-06	Dec-10	$\Delta SAS = 0.215 + 0.112*\Delta prec_{2ma} + 0.316*(p-pet)_{2ma}$	1.11	1.86	0.61
PZ-I	GW	Jan-06	Dec-10	$\Delta SAS = \exp(1.85 + 0.203*\ln(p-pet)_{2ma}+10) + 0.0106*\Delta prec_{2ma}) - 10$	1.07	2.45	0.54
PZ-J	GW	Jan-06	Dec-10	$\Delta SAS = -1.01 + 0.236*prec_{2ma} + 0.133*\Delta(p-pet)_{2ma}$	1.25	1.97	0.64
PZ-M	GW	Jan-06	Dec-10	$\Delta SAS = -0.790 + 0.186*prec_{2ma} + 0.138*\Delta(p-pet)_{2ma}$	1.25	2.06	0.60
PZ-N	GW	Jan-06	Dec-10	$\Delta SAS = -0.702 + 0.160*prec_{2ma} + 0.115*\Delta(p-pet)_{2ma}$	1.25	2.25	0.33
PZ-O	GW	Jan-06	Dec-10	$\Delta SAS = -2.91 + 0.159*prec_{2ma} +1.00*\ln(p-pet)_{2ma} + 10)$	1.94	2.00	0.50
PZ-P	GW	Jan-06	Dec-10	$\Delta SAS = \exp(2.23 + 0.0593*\ln(prec_{2ma}) + 0.00376*\Delta(p-pet)) - 10$	1.00	1.69	0.55
PZ-Q	GW	Jan-06	Dec-10	$\Delta SAS = \exp(2.01 + 0.133*\ln((p-pet)_{2ma} + 10) + 0.009*\Delta(p-pet)_{2ma}) - 10$	1.20	1.65	0.44
Scoggin Lake	SW	May-05	Dec-08	$\Delta WL = \exp(2.65 + 0.0105*prec_{2ma} - 0.0137*Q_{2ma}) - 10$	1.03	1.90	0.41
Coon Pond	SW	Sep-01	Aug-06	$\Delta WL = -0.0905 + 0.0237*\Delta prec + 0.146*(p-pet)_{2ma}$	1.01	1.94	0.70
Indian Lake	SW	Jul-99	Dec-08	$\Delta WL = \exp(2.61 + 0.0109*prec_{2ma} - 0.0117*Q_{2ma}) - 10$	1.04	2.15	0.70

Table 6b. Computed p-values for the explanatory variables associated with the regression equations in table 6a.

[UFA, Upper Floridan aquifer; SAS, surficial aquifer system; GW, groundwater monitoring site; SW, surface-water monitoring site; $prec$, monthly precipitation, in inches; $prec_{2ma}$, 2-month moving average of $prec$, in inches; $\Delta prec$, monthly change in precipitation, in inches; $\Delta prec_{2ma}$, 2-month moving average of change in $prec$, in inches; pet, monthly potential evapotranspiration, in inches; $(p\text{-}pet)_{2ma}$, 2-month moving average of the difference between $prec$ and pet, in inches; $\Delta(p\text{-}pet)$, change in $(p\text{-}pet)$, in inches; $\Delta(p\text{-}pet)_{2ma}$, 2-month moving average of change in $(p\text{-}pet)$, in inches; Q, monthly groundwater pumpage from municipal supply wells located within 12 miles of the site; Q_{2ma}, 2-month moving average of pumpage, in million gallons per day; ΔQ, monthly change in pumpage, in million gallons per day; ΔQ_{2ma}, 2-month moving average of change in pumpage, in million gallons per day; SIV, stressor influence value; ns, not significant given the other terms in the model. Available periods of record are shown in table 6a]

Project site	Site type	Explanatory variable included in best regressed equation											SIV[1]
		$prec$	$prec_{2ma}$	$\Delta prec$	$\Delta prec_{2ma}$	$(p\text{-}pet)_{2ma}$	$\Delta(p\text{-}pet)$	$\Delta(p\text{-}pet)_{2ma}$	Q	Q_{2ma}	ΔQ	ΔQ_{2ma}	
Tiger Bay 4A UFA	GW	ns	ns	ns	<0.001	<0.001	ns	ns	ns	ns	<0.001	ns	3
Tomoka tower SAS	GW	ns	<0.001	ns	<0.001	ns	ns	ns	ns	0.016	ns	ns	2
Tomoka tower UFA	GW	ns	<0.001	ns	ns	ns	ns	ns	ns	ns	ns	<0.001	3
SR40 SAS	GW	ns	<0.001	ns	<0.001	ns	ns	ns	ns	ns	ns	ns	1
SR40 UFA	GW	ns	<0.001	ns	ns	ns	ns	ns	ns	ns	ns	ns	1
Indian Lake site 3 SAS	GW	ns	<0.001	ns	ns	ns	ns	ns	ns	0.031	ns	ns	2
Indian Lake site 350 SAS	GW	<0.001	ns	ns	0.003	ns	ns	ns	ns	ns	ns	ns	1
Union Camp SAS	GW	ns	ns	ns	<.001	<0.001	ns	ns	ns	ns	ns	0.001	2
PZ-A	GW	ns	<0.001	ns	<.001	ns	ns	ns	0.040	ns	ns	ns	2
PZ-F	GW	ns	ns	ns	0.012	<0.001	ns	ns	ns	ns	ns	ns	1
PZ-I	GW	ns	ns	ns	0.005	<0.001	ns	ns	ns	ns	ns	ns	1
PZ-J	GW	ns	<0.001	ns	ns	ns	ns	0.002	ns	ns	ns	ns	1
PZ-M	GW	ns	<0.001	ns	ns	ns	ns	0.001	ns	ns	ns	ns	1
PZ-N	GW	ns	0.001	ns	ns	ns	ns	0.043	ns	ns	ns	ns	1
PZ-O	GW	ns	0.001	ns	ns	0.028	0.005	ns	ns	ns	ns	ns	1
PZ-P	GW	ns	<0.001	ns	ns	ns	ns	ns	ns	ns	ns	ns	1
PZ-Q	GW	ns	ns	ns	ns	<0.001	ns	0.011	ns	ns	ns	ns	1
Scoggin Lake	SW	ns	<0.001	ns	ns	ns	ns	ns	ns	<.001	ns	ns	3
Coon Pond	SW	ns	ns	0.002	ns	<0.001	ns	ns	ns	ns	ns	ns	1
Indian Lake	SW	ns	<0.001	ns	ns	<.001	ns	ns	ns	<.001	ns	ns	3

[1] Explanation for stressor influence value (SIV) based on comparison of coefficient p-values

1 Water-level changes are correlated with precipitation but not with pumpage

2 Water-level changes are more highly correlated with precipitation than with pumpage

3 Water-level changes are highly correlated with both precipitation and pumpage.

4 Water-level changes are more highly correlated with pumpage than with precipitation

5 Water-level changes are correlated with pumpage but not with precipitation.

Although changes in SAS water levels were correlated with groundwater withdrawals at three of the five monitoring-well sites, SAS water-level changes were correlated solely with precipitation at all but one (PZ-A) of the nine piezometer sites (table 6b). The reason(s) for the more persistent influence of withdrawals on groundwater-level changes measured in the SAS at the monitoring-well sites is unclear. However, the screened intervals at the monitoring-well sites penetrate deeper into the SAS than those in the piezometers (table 1). Consequently, a thinner sequence of sediments vertically separate the pumped UFA aquifer from the interval in the SAS being monitored by these wells. Also, the deeper part of the SAS breached by the monitoring wells may be composed of low-permeability sediments not breached by the shallower piezometers. Low permeable sediments serve to decrease the degree of the hydraulic connection between the two aquifers. Similarly, PZ-A is the deepest of the nine piezometers which may help to explain why it is the only piezometer where water-level changes are correlated with groundwater withdrawals.

Water-level changes at Scoggin and Indian Lakes were found to be highly correlated with precipitation and groundwater withdrawals. These results are somewhat unexpected, as lake stage changes were expected to function more like those measured at the SAS sites; instead, stage changes responded more like those measured in the UFA at Tiger Bay 4A UFA and Tomoka tower UFA. That is, changes at the lake sites were more highly correlated with groundwater withdrawals than were changes at nearby SAS sites. These results indicate that the lakes may be better connected hydraulically to the UFA than is the surrounding SAS. Whereas the SAS and UFA are presumably separated by a relatively intact confining unit at the groundwater-monitoring sites, the unit beneath these karstic lakes may have been breached in the geologic past. Karst collapse can provide flow paths for vertical movement of water between the two aquifers (Kindinger and others, 2000; Cunningham and Walker, 2009). At Indian Lake, seismic-reflection profiles indicate that two areas of subsidence exist below the lake bottom, and that "There appears to be an area of collapse within the Ocala (limestone), approximately 150-meters wide, that has caused a concomitant subsidence in the southern part of the lake" (Kindinger and others, 2000). The report adds that "In the uppermost part of the profiles, a relatively transparent signal characteristic of organic debris and sands appear to be infilling the depressions."

Regression results were improved for a number of sites by log-transforming response and explanatory variables. At PZ-P, for example, transformation of the response variable improved the distribution of residuals to better comply with the normality assumption (fig. 9a). Prior to transformation, the Kolmogorov test (Conover, 1999) indicated that the residuals were not normally distributed about the mean (p-value of less than 0.01), but were normally distributed after transformation (p-value equal to 0.05). At Tomoka tower UFA, log-transformation of the precipitation variable served to linearize the relations with water-level changes as depicted in the partial residuals plot in figure 9b. As expected and typical of all the partial plots examined in these analyses, changes in water levels at Tomoka Tower UFA are directly related to precipitation and inversely related to groundwater withdrawals. Also, the scatter of the residuals appears to conform with the assumption of homoscedasticity.

Measured and model-predicted water-level changes were contrasted to evaluate predictive applications of the models (fig. 10). Among nonpiezometer sites, R^2 determined from simple linear regression varied from 0.41 at Scoggin Lake to 0.81 at Tomoka tower SAS. For each model, the slope of the line of best fit is less than 1.0 (dashed line of equality), indicating that water-level changes predicted by the best regressed equations underestimated measured values, particularly for large water-level changes of greater than 1.0 ft. Large water-level changes are associated with months of high rainfall, typically greater than 10 in., which were identified as points in the analyses that produced large standardized residuals or observations of high leverage. These results indicate that the MLR models developed in this study may provide better predictive results when applied to periods of average (or below average) precipitation conditions than for wetter conditions.

Analyses of Water-Level Changes between May 2000 and June 2007

The previous analyses accounted for the full POR available at each site to include as many observations as possible. However, because the PORs for the 11 monitoring well and lake sites are variable, results from one site to the next cannot be easily compared because varying patterns of precipitation and groundwater withdrawals affect relations with the response variable. To allow for cross comparison of results, a common period of record from May 2000 to June 2007 was identified for analyses. This 2.2-year (86-month) POR was selected because it is the longest period common to the majority of the sites. This POR contains drought and wet conditions and, based on precipitation measured at the Daytona Beach NOAA station, is assumed to be representative of averaged conditions. Long-term precipitation at Daytona Beach averaged 4.1 in/mo between 1949 and 2008 compared with 4.38 in/mo between May 2000 and June 2007.

Explanatory variables account for 60 percent or more of the variance in water-level changes at four of the seven sites, and ranged from 73 percent at Indian Lake to 40 percent at SR40 UFA (table 7a). All VIF values are less than 2.0, indicating that multicollinearity among explanatory variables is not statistically significant. Calculated D_L values are below associated threshold values reported in table A.6 of Montgomery and Peck (1982), indicating that no statistical evidence exists that the residuals are serially correlated. $Prec_{2ma}$ and $\Delta prec_{2ma}$ were the two climatic variables most commonly included in the regression models, whereas Q_{2ma} and ΔQ_{2ma} were the anthropogenic variables exhibiting the most common influence on water-level changes.

A. Frequency histogram of residuals for PZ-P

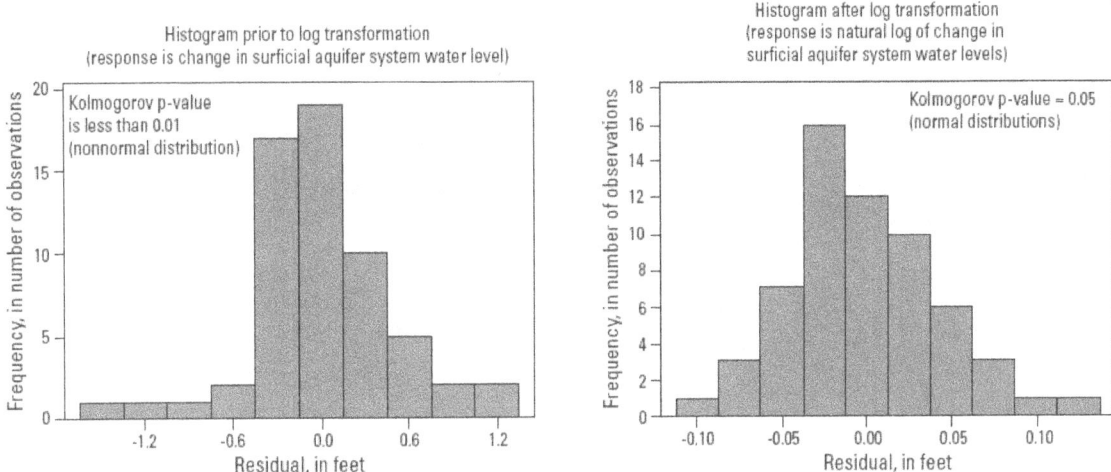

B. Partial residuals of water-level change and explanatory variables for Tomoka Tower UFA

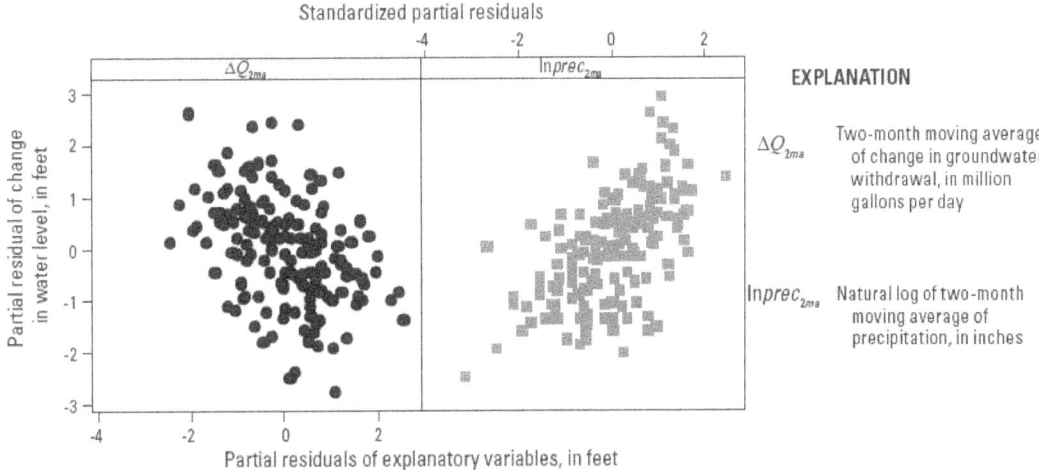

Figure 9. *A,* Frequency of residuals in water-level changes at piezometer site PZ-P prior to and following log-transformation of the response variable, 2006–2010; and *B,* standardized partial residuals of water-level change and explanatory variables at Tomoka tower Upper Floridan aquifer, 1996–2008.

Water-level changes at all but the two SR40 sites are statistically correlated with both precipitation and groundwater withdrawals (table 7b). The three sites closest to areas of concentrated withdrawals (Tiger Bay 4A UFA, Tomoka tower UFA, and Indian Lake) are highly correlated with precipitation and withdrawals (SIV = 3), whereas water-level changes at Scoggin Lake and Union Camp SAS, which are further removed from groundwater withdrawals, are more highly correlated with precipitation than with withdrawals (SIV = 2). Changes in the UFA and SAS water levels at SR40, located about 6 mi from the nearest pumping well, were correlated solely with precipitation (SIV = 1).

The SIVs determined for the May 2000 to June 2007 POR (table 7b) are comparable to those documented for the available PORs (table 6b). Only one of the seven sites (Scoggin Lake) included in the May 2000 to June 2007 analyses had an SIV that differed from that determined across its available POR. Water-level changes at Indian Lake again responded similarly to the UFA sites; that is, changes in lake stage were highly correlated with both groundwater withdrawals and precipitation (SIV = 3), as were changes at Tiger Bay 4A UFA and Tomoka tower UFA.

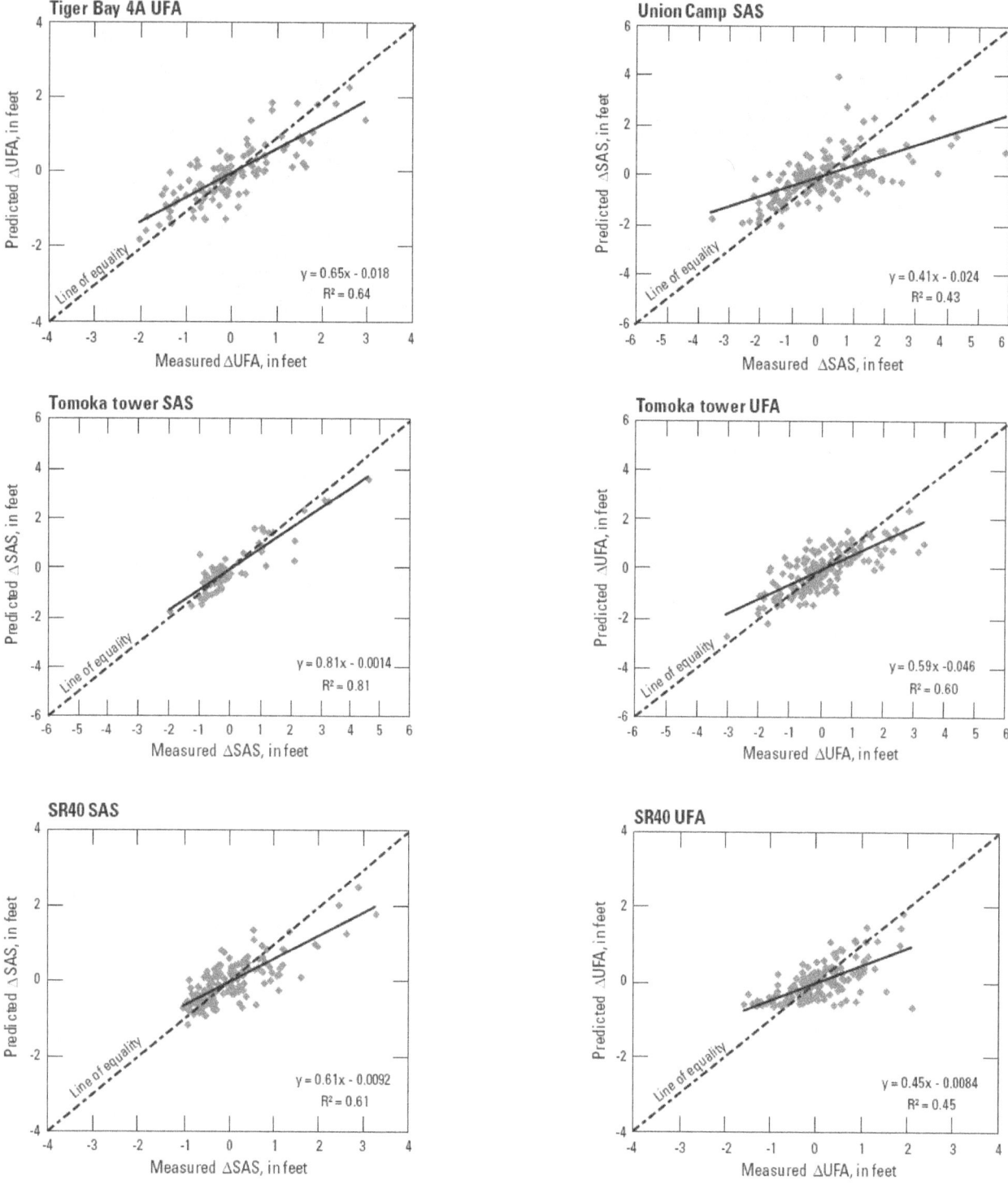

Figure 10.   Measured and predicted monthly water-level changes at the monitoring well and lake sites across available periods of record.

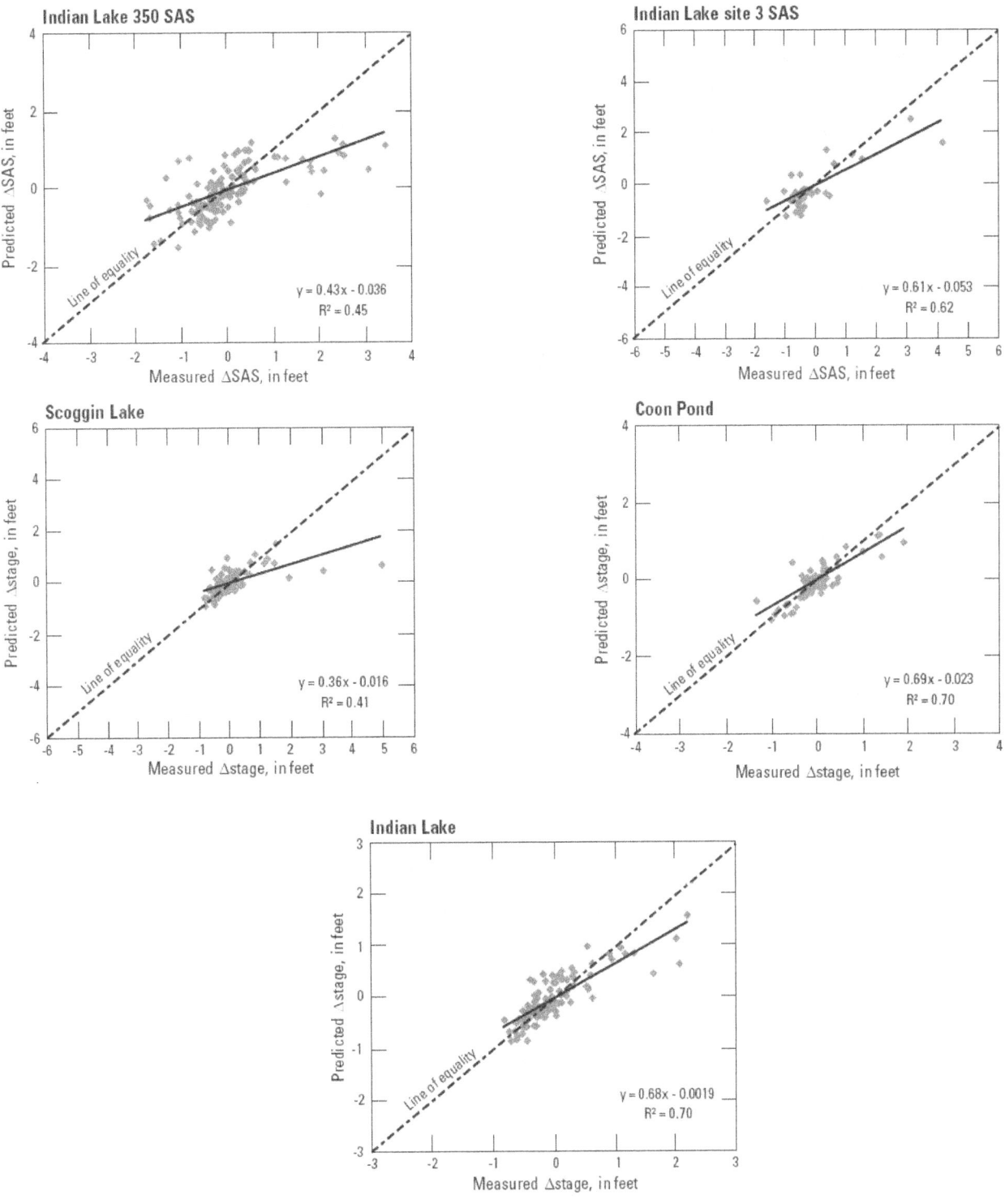

Figure 10. Measured and predicted monthly water-level changes at the monitoring well and lake sites across available periods of record. —Continued

Table 7a. Regression equations chosen to model the change in water levels at selected groundwater and lake monitoring sites, May 2000–June 2007.

[UFA, Upper Floridan aquifer; SAS, surficial aquifer system; VIF, variance inflation factor; D_L, Durbin statistic; R^2_{adj}, adjusted coefficient of determination; $prec$, monthly precipitation, in inches; $prec_{2ma}$, 2-month moving average of prec, in inches; $\Delta prec_{2ma}$, 2-month moving average of change in $prec$, in inches; pet, potential evapotranspiration, in inches; p-pet, monthly difference between $prec$ and pet, in inches; $(p$-$pet)_{2ma}$, 2-month moving average of the difference between the $prec$ and pet, in inches; Q, monthly pumpage, in million gallons per day; Q_{2ma}, 2-month moving average of pumpage, in million gallons per day; ΔQ, monthly change in pumpage, in million gallons per day; ΔQ_{2ma}, 2-month moving average of change in pumpage, in million gallons per day]

Project site	Best regressed equation	VIF	D_L	R^2_{adj}
Tiger Bay 4A UFA	$\Delta UFA = 5.68 + 0.0942*prec + 0.102*\Delta prec_{2ma} - 0.215*Q$	2.03	2.00	0.66
Tokoma tower UFA	$\Delta UFA = \exp\left(2.89 + 0.153*\ln\left((p\text{-}pet)_{2ma} + 10\right) - 0.408*\ln\left(\Delta Q_{2ma} + 10\right)\right) - 10$	1 33	2.21	0.60
SR40 SAS	$\Delta SAS = -0.740 + 0.168*prec_{2ma} + 0.0910*\Delta prec_{2ma}$	1 23	1.99	0.66
SR40 UFA	$\Delta UFA = -0.651 + 0.148*prec_{2ma}$	1.00	1.79	0.40
Union Camp SAS	$\Delta SAS = \exp\left(1.95 + 0.161*\ln\left((p\text{-}pet)_{2ma} + 10\right) + 0.0174*\Delta prec_{2ma} - 0.0476*\Delta Q_{2ma}\right) - 10$	1 26	1.94	0.43
Scoggin Lake	$\Delta WL = \exp\left(2.56 + 0.0094*prec_{2ma} - 0.0107*Q_{2ma}\right) - 10$	1.06	1.99	0.46
Indian Lake	$\Delta WL = \exp\left(2.58 + 0.0112*prec_{2ma} - 0.0108*Q_{2ma}\right) - 10$	1.08	2.00	0.73

Table 7b. Computed p-values for explanatory variables associated with the regression equations in table 7a, May 2000–June 2007.

[UFA, Upper Floridan aquifer; SAS, surficial aquifer system; SIV, stressor influence value; $prec$, monthly precipitation, in inches; $prec_{2ma}$, 2-month moving average of prec, in inches; $\Delta prec_{2ma}$, 2-month moving average of change in $prec$, in inches; $(p$-$pet)_{2ma}$, 2-month moving average of the difference between the $prec$ and pet, in inches; Q, monthly pumpage, in million gallons per day; Q_{2ma}, 2-month moving average of pumpage, in million gallons per day; ΔQ_{2ma}, 2-month moving average of change in pumpage, in million gallons per day; <, less than; ns, not significant, given other terms in the model]

Project site	Explanatory variable included in best regressed equation							SIV[1]
	$prec$	$prec_{2ma}$	$\Delta prec_{2ma}$	$(p\text{-}pet)_{2ma}$	Q	Q_{2ma}	ΔQ_{2ma}	
Tiger Bay 4A UFA	<0.001	ns	0.001	ns	<0.001	ns	ns	3
Tokoma tower UFA	ns	ns	ns	<0.001	ns	ns	<0.001	3
SR40 SAS	ns	<0.001	<0.001	ns	ns	ns	ns	1
SR40 UFA	ns	<0.001	ns	ns	ns	ns	ns	1
Union Camp SAS	ns	ns	<0.001	<0.001	ns	ns	0.001	2
Scoggin Lake	ns	<0.001	ns	ns	ns	0.002	ns	2
Indian Lake	ns	<0.001	ns	ns	ns	<0.001	ns	3

[1]Explanation for stressor influence value (SIV) based on comparison of coefficient p-values.

1   Water-level changes are correlated with precipitation but not with pumpage.

2   Water-level changes are more highly correlated with precipitation than with pumpage.

3   Water-level changes are highly correlated with both precipitation and pumpage.

4   Water-level changes are more highly correlated with pumpage than with precipitation.

5   Water-level changes are correlated with pumpage but not with precipitation.

Analyses of Water-Level Changes by Season

Precipitation and groundwater-withdrawal conditions change on a seasonal basis. Seasons are defined for this study on a calendar rather than astronomical (equinox or solstice) basis. Winter months include December, January, and February; spring months include March, April, and May; summer months include June, July, and August; and fall months include September, October, and November. Water-level changes used in the seasonal analyses were calculated in the same fashion as those for the previous analyses; that is, by subtracting the previous month's average water level from that of the current month. For example, changes in water levels for the spring months of March, April, and May were calculated by subtracting the average February water level from the average March water level, the average March water level from the average April water level, and the average April water level from the average May water level, respectively. Only those six sites having at least 10 years of available record were included in these analyses.

Changes in water levels, the amount of available water (Δ(prec-PET)), and groundwater withdrawals exhibit distinct seasonal variations (table 8). Water levels declined at all sites (negative values) over the drier winter and spring months but increased at all but one site during the summer and fall months (positive values). Variations in precipitation and withdrawals may help to qualitatively explain these seasonal contrasts. When averaged for the six sites, water-level declines were greatest during the spring (-0.52 foot per month, ft/mo), the season having the greatest average monthly increase in groundwater withdrawals (0.69 Mgal/d), as well as the highest average monthly reduction in available water (-1.70 in/mo). By contrast, water levels recovered by an average of 0.42 ft/mo during the summer months, concurrent with the largest seasonal increase in available water (1.91 in/mo) and decrease in groundwater withdrawals (-0.41 Mgal/d). Moreover, water levels continued to recover in the fall (0.19 ft/mo) despite a decrease in the amount of available water (-0.30 in/mo). These water-level increases are probably due, in part, to the continued reductions in groundwater withdrawals (-0.29 Mgal/d) that occurred over the fall months.

Explanatory variables included in the regression models accounted for greater than 60 percent of the variance in water-level changes in 8 of the 24 seasonal analyses at the six sites (table 9a). Among all regression models, the R^2_{adj} values ranged from 0.83 at Tiger Bay 4A UFA in the fall to 0.09 at SR40 UFA in the winter. Lowest R^2_{adj} values generally occurred in the winter months when the stresses imposed by low rainfall and increased groundwater withdrawals were minimal. At SR40

Table 8. Average monthly change in water levels, available water, and municipal pumpage for each of the four seasons.

[UFA, Upper Floridan aquifer; SAS, surficial aquifer system; Δ(p-pet), monthly change in the difference between precipitation and potential evapotranspiration (available water), in inches; ΔQ, monthly change in pumpage, in million gallons per day. *Note:* Negative values represent average monthly decreases whereas positive values represent average monthly increases]

Project site	Winter[1]	Spring[2]	Summer[3]	Fall[4]
	Average monthly change in water level, in feet			
Tiger Bay 4A UFA	-0.08	-0.58	0.29	0.16
Tomoka tower UFA	-0.27	-0.82	0.44	0.61
SR40 SAS	-0.29	-0.12	0.12	0.19
SR40 UFA	-0.25	-0.34	0.30	0.22
Indian Lake 350 SAS	-0.13	-0.49	0.68	-0.06
Union Camp SAS	-0.01	-0.75	0.69	0.01
Average monthly water-level change, in feet	-0.17	-0.52	0.42	0.19
Average monthly change in available water Δ(p-pet), in inches per month	0.03	-1.70	1.91	-0.30
Average monthly change in pumpage ΔQ, in million gallons per day	0.09	0.69	-0.41	-0.29

[1]December, January, February.

[2]March, April, May.

[3]June, July, August.

[4]September, October, November.

Table 9a.   Regression equations chosen to model seasonal changes in water levels at selected groundwater and lake monitoring sites.

[UFA, Upper Floridan aquifer; SAS, surficial aquifer system; VIF, variance inflation factor; D_L, Durbin statistic; R^2_{adj}, adjusted coefficient of determination; $prec$, monthly precipitation, in inches; $prec_{2ma}$, 2-month moving average of $prec$, in inches; $\Delta prec_{2ma}$, 2-month moving average of change in $prec$, in inches; pet, potential evapotranspiration, in inches; p-pet, difference between $prec$ and potential evapotranspiration, in inches; $(p$-$pet)_{2ma}$, 2-month moving average of the difference between $prec$ and potential evapotranspiration, in inches; ΔQ, monthly change in pumpage, in million gallons per day; ΔQ_{2ma}, 2-month moving average of change in pumpage, in million gallons per day. Available periods of record used in analyses are shown in table 1]

Project site	Best regressed equation	VIF	D_L	R^2_{adj}
Winter (December, January, February)				
Tiger Bay 4A UFA	ΔUFA $= -4.03 + 1.70*\ln((p\text{-}pet)+10)$	1.00	2.19	0.43
Tokoma tower UFA	ΔUFA $= -0.242 + 0.209*(p\text{-}pet)_{2ma} - 0.226*\Delta Q$	1.01	2.20	0.55
SR40 SAS	ΔSAS $= -0.928 + 0.253*prec_{2ma}$	1.00	2.52	0.53
SR40 UFA	ΔUFA $= -0.128 + 0.150*\Delta prec_{2ma}$	1.00	2.40	0.09
Indian Lake site 350 SAS	ΔSAS $= -0.536 + 0.143*prec$	1.00	1.68	0.80
Union Camp SAS	ΔSAS $= -0.302 + 0.455*\ln(prec_{2ma}) + 0.158*\Delta prec_{2ma}$	1.15	2.44	0.26
Spring (March, April, May)				
Tiger Bay 4A UFA	ΔUFA $= \exp(2.33 + 0.0206*(p\text{-}pet)_{2ma} - 0.0454*\Delta Q) - 10$	1.01	2.39	0.62
Tokoma tower UFA	ΔUFA $= \exp(2.15 + 0.100*\ln(prec_{2ma}) - 0.0166*\Delta Q) - 10$	1.05	2.43	0.67
SR40 SAS	ΔSAS $= \exp(2.25 + 0.0134*prec_{2ma} + 0.0140*\Delta prec_{2ma}) - 10$	1.31	2.03	0.48
SR40 UFA	ΔUFA $= \exp(2.01 + 0.133*\ln((p\text{-}pet)_{2ma}+10)) - 10$	1.00	2.21	0.52
Indian Lake site 350 SAS	ΔSAS $= \exp(1.98 + 0.153*\ln((p\text{-}pet)_{2ma}+10) - 0.0397*\Delta Q) - 10$	1.03	1.86	0.55
Union Camp SAS	ΔSAS $= \exp(1.44 + 0.321*\ln(\Delta prec_{2ma}+10) + 0.0177*prec_{2ma}) - 10$	1.22	2.63	0.44
Summer (June, July, August)				
Tiger Bay 4A UFA	ΔUFA $= \exp(3.33 + 0.0195*\Delta((p\text{-}pet)_{2ma}+10) - 0.0354*Q) - 10$	1.18	2.16	0.58
Tokoma tower UFA	ΔUFA $= \exp(1.85 + 0.223*\ln((p\text{-}pet)_{2ma}+10)) - 10$	1.00	1.80	0.46
SR40 SAS	ΔSAS $= \exp(2.18 + 0.0236*prec_{2ma}) - 10$	1.00	2.56	0.63
SR40 UFA	ΔUFA $= -1.24 + 0.854*\ln(prec_{2ma}) - 0.913*\Delta Q_{2ma}$	1.14	2.25	0.76
Indian Lake site 350 SAS	ΔSAS $= \exp(2.16 + 0.107*\ln(prec)) - 10$	1.00	2.21	0.36
Union Camp SAS	ΔSAS $= \exp(2.01 + 0.192*\ln(prec_{2ma}) - 0.144*\Delta Q_{2ma}) - 10$	1.09	1.89	0.55
Fall (September, October, November)				
Tiger Bay 4A UFA	ΔUFA $= 6.23 + 0.636*\ln(prec) - 3.04*\ln(\Delta Q+10)$	1.39	1.96	0.83
Tokoma tower UFA	ΔUFA $= \exp(2.28 + 0.00948*prec - 0.0485*\Delta Q_{2ma}) - 10$	1.40	1.86	0.50
SR40 SAS	ΔSAS $= 0.095 + 0.103*\Delta prec_{2ma} + 0.204*(p\text{-}pet)_{2ma} - 0.563*\Delta Q$	1.54	2.01	0.73
SR40 UFA	ΔUFA $= -0.637 + 0.136*prec_{2ma} - 0.663*\Delta Q_{2ma}$	1.19	1.69	0.71
Indian Lake site 350 SAS	ΔSAS $= \exp(3.03 - 0.325*\ln(\Delta Q+10)) - 10$	1.00	2.32	0.40
Union Camp SAS	ΔSAS $= \exp(2.14 + 0.0791*\ln(prec_{2ma}) - 0.0938*\Delta Q_{2ma}) - 10$	1.21	1.85	0.46

Table 9b. Computed p-values for the explanatory variables associated with the regression equations in table 9a.

[UFA, Upper Floridan aquifer; SAS, surficial aquifer system; SIV, stressor influence value; *prec*, monthly precipitation, in inches; $prec_{2ma}$, 2-month moving average of *prec*, in inches; $\Delta prec_{2ma}$, 2-month moving average of change in *prec*, in inches; *pet*, potential evapotranspiration, in inches; *p-pet*, monthly difference between *prec* and *pet*, in inches; $(p\text{-}pet)_{2ma}$, 2-month moving average of the difference between *prec* and *pet*, in inches; $\Delta(p\text{-}pet)_{2ma}$, 2-month moving average of change in the difference between *prec* and *pet*, in inches; *Q*, monthly pumpage, in million gallons per day; ΔQ, monthly change in pumpage, in million gallons per day; ΔQ_{2ma}, 2-month moving average of change in pumpage, in million gallons per day; ns, not significant, given other terms in the model. Available periods of record used in analyses are shown in table 1]

Project site	Explanatory variable included in best regressed equation									
	prec	$prec_{2ma}$	$\Delta prec_{2ma}$	*p-pet*	$(p\text{-}pet)_{2ma}$	$\Delta(p\text{-}pet)_{2ma}$	*Q*	ΔQ	ΔQ_{2ma}	SIV[1]
Winter (December–January–February)										
Tiger Bay 4A UFA	ns	ns	ns	<0.001	ns	ns	ns	ns	ns	1
Tomoka tower UFA	ns	ns	ns	ns	<0.001	ns	ns	<0.001	ns	3
SR40 SAS	ns	<0.001	ns	ns	ns	ns	ns	ns	ns	1
SR40 UFA	ns	ns	0.031	ns	ns	ns	ns	ns	ns	1
Indian Lake 350 SAS	<0.001	ns	ns	ns	ns	ns	ns	ns	ns	1
Union Camp SAS	ns	0.039	0.046	ns	ns	ns	ns	ns	ns	1
Spring (March–April–May)									**Average SIV =**	1.3
Tiger Bay 4A UFA	ns	ns	ns	ns	<0.001	ns	ns	<0.001	ns	3
Tomoka tower UFA	ns	<0.001	ns	ns	ns	ns	ns	0.045	ns	2
SR40 SAS	ns	0.003	0.004	ns	ns	ns	ns	ns	ns	1
SR40 UFA	ns	ns	ns	ns	<0.001	ns	ns	ns	ns	1
Indian Lake 350 SAS	ns	ns	ns	ns	<0.001	ns	ns	0.004	ns	2
Union Camp SAS	ns	0.036	<0.001	ns	ns	ns	ns	ns	ns	1
Summer (June–July–August)									**Average SIV =**	1.7
Tiger Bay 4A UFA	ns	ns	ns	ns	ns	0.001	0.005	ns	ns	2
Tomoka tower UFA	ns	ns	ns	ns	<0.001	ns	ns	ns	ns	1
SR40 SAS	ns	<0.001	ns	ns	ns	ns	ns	ns	ns	1
SR40 UFA	ns	<0.001	ns	ns	ns	ns	ns	ns	0.001	2
Indian Lake 350 SAS	<0.001	ns	ns	ns	ns	ns	ns	ns	ns	1
Union Camp SAS	ns	<0.001	ns	ns	ns	ns	ns	ns	0.001	2
Fall (September–October–November)									**Average SIV =**	1.5
Tiger Bay 4A UFA	<0.001	ns	ns	ns	ns	ns	ns	<0.001	ns	3
Tomoka tower UFA	0.004	ns	ns	ns	ns	ns	ns	ns	0.003	3
SR40 SAS	ns	ns	0.004	ns	<0.001	ns	ns	0.020	ns	2
SR40 UFA	ns	<0.001	ns	ns	ns	ns	ns	ns	0.006	2
Indian Lake 350 SAS	ns	ns	ns	ns	ns	ns	ns	<0.001	ns	5
Union Camp SAS	ns	0.002	ns	ns	ns	ns	ns	ns	0.006	2
									Average SIV =	2.8

[1]Explanation for stressor influence value (SIV) based on comparison of coefficient p-values.

1   Water-level changes are correlated with precipitation but not with pumpage.

2   Water-level changes are more highly correlated with precipitation than with pumpage.

3   Water-level changes are highly correlated with both precipitation and pumpage.

4   Water-level changes are more highly correlated with pumpage than with precipitation.

5   Water-level changes are correlated with pumpage but not with precipitation.

UFA, the relatively high degree of unexplained error may be attributed, at least in part, to the effects of short-lived, high rates of agricultural withdrawals needed for winter freeze protection, a stress not accounted for in the analyses. All VIF values were less than 2.0, indicating insignificant multicollinearity among explanatory variables (table 9a). Calculated D_L values were below associated threshold values reported in table A.6 of Montgomery and Peck (1982), indicating no statistical evidence of serial correlation among the data (table 9a).

Climatic variables most commonly included in the seasonal models were the 2-month moving averages of precipitation ($prec_{2ma}$) and available water ($p\text{-}pet)_{2ma}$, whereas the monthly and 2-month moving averages of change in groundwater withdrawals (ΔQ and ΔQ_{2ma}) were the anthropogenic variables most common to the models. Water-level changes at most sites were least correlated with groundwater withdrawals in the winter and summer months, and were most highly correlated with withdrawals in the fall and spring (table 9b). Reduced rates of groundwater withdrawals probably contributed to increased (recovered) water levels in the fall, whereas increased rates of withdrawal probably contributed to water-level declines in the spring (table 8). When averaged for the six sites, SIVs range from 1.3 in the winter, when water-level changes were correlated solely with precipitation at five of the six sites, to 2.8 in the fall, when changes were statistically correlated with groundwater withdrawals at all six sites.

Analyses of Drought-Affected Water-Level Changes

This section examines the relative influences of precipitation and groundwater withdrawals on changes in water levels during an extended period of drought which occurred in central Florida between October 2005 and June 2008. This period can be clearly identified from a plot of the long-term (1949 to 2008) cumulative rainfall departure curve developed for the Daytona Beach NOAA rainfall station (fig. 11). The slopes depicted on this curve are useful for identifying extended wet and dry hydrologic conditions between 1995 and 2008. A rising slope, for example, identifies a period of above average rainfall whereas a declining slope reflects below average rainfall. The declining slope in the curve between October 2005 and June 2008 is indicative of a drought reflected by the declining water levels shown previously in figure 4. Six sites have PORs that include the full period of drought.

Explanatory variables account for greater than 60 percent of the variance in water-level changes at five of the six sites. The lowest R^2_{adj} (0.51) was computed for the data from Union Camp SAS, and the highest R^2_{adj} (0.81) was computed for the data from Indian Lake (table 10a). When compared with precipitation-averaged conditions (tables 6a, 7a), the relatively high values of R^2_{adj} determined for Indian and Scoggin Lakes (0.81 and 0.75) indicate that monthly changes in stage during

the drought were well explained by the variables included in the best regressed equations. It is possible that overland runoff, which contributed water to the lakes during wetter periods within the precipitation-averaged PORs, introduced some degree of nonlinearity or unexplained error in the relations between stage and precipitation. The absence of runoff during drought conditions may serve to minimize such error.

All VIF values were less than 2.0, indicating no significant multicollinearity among explanatory variables. Similarly, D_L values indicate no evidence of either positive or negative serial correlation.

Groundwater withdrawals were less correlated with water-level changes at sites further removed from municipal well fields (SR40 UFA and Union Camp SAS) than at sites located closer to areas of concentrated withdrawals (Tomoka tower SAS and UFA). These relations are similar to those previously discussed for precipitation-averaged conditions. Also, water-level changes at Indian and Scoggin Lakes were more were highly correlated with groundwater withdrawals (SIV = 3) than were changes measured at both of the nearby Tomoka tower sites (SIV = 2). On average, groundwater-withdrawal rates during droughts (table 10a) are greater than those measured over precipitation-averaged PORs (fig. 7).

Comparison of Regression Results

Comparison of SIVs determined from previously discussed analyses is useful for making generalized observations about relations between water-level changes, precipitation, and groundwater withdrawals (table 11). Overall, results are consistent with those that may have been expected, given the placements and targeted monitoring zones of the well sites. That is, water-level changes measured at sites tapping the UFA, the source of groundwater withdrawals, were more highly correlated with withdrawals than were water-level changes measured at sites that tap the unpumped SAS. Also, water-level changes tended to be less correlated with groundwater withdrawals, and more highly or solely correlated with precipitation, at sites further removed from municipal well fields. The SIVs determined for Indian and Scoggin Lakes, regardless of the temporal scale of the PORs, are more comparable to those determined for the UFA monitoring sites than for the SAS sites. These results indicate that these lakes may be better connected hydraulically with the underlying UFA than the SAS is at the groundwater sites.

The percentage of variance in water-level changes accounted for by explanatory variables can be related to the relative influence of groundwater withdrawals. When averaged for sites common to each analyses, the lowest value of R^2_{adj} (0.44), determined from the winter season analyses, is associated with the lowest SIV (1.3). Conversely, the two highest averaged values of R^2_{adj} (0.67 and 0.61), determined from the drought and fall seasonal analyses, are associated with the two highest SIVs (2.0 and 2.8).

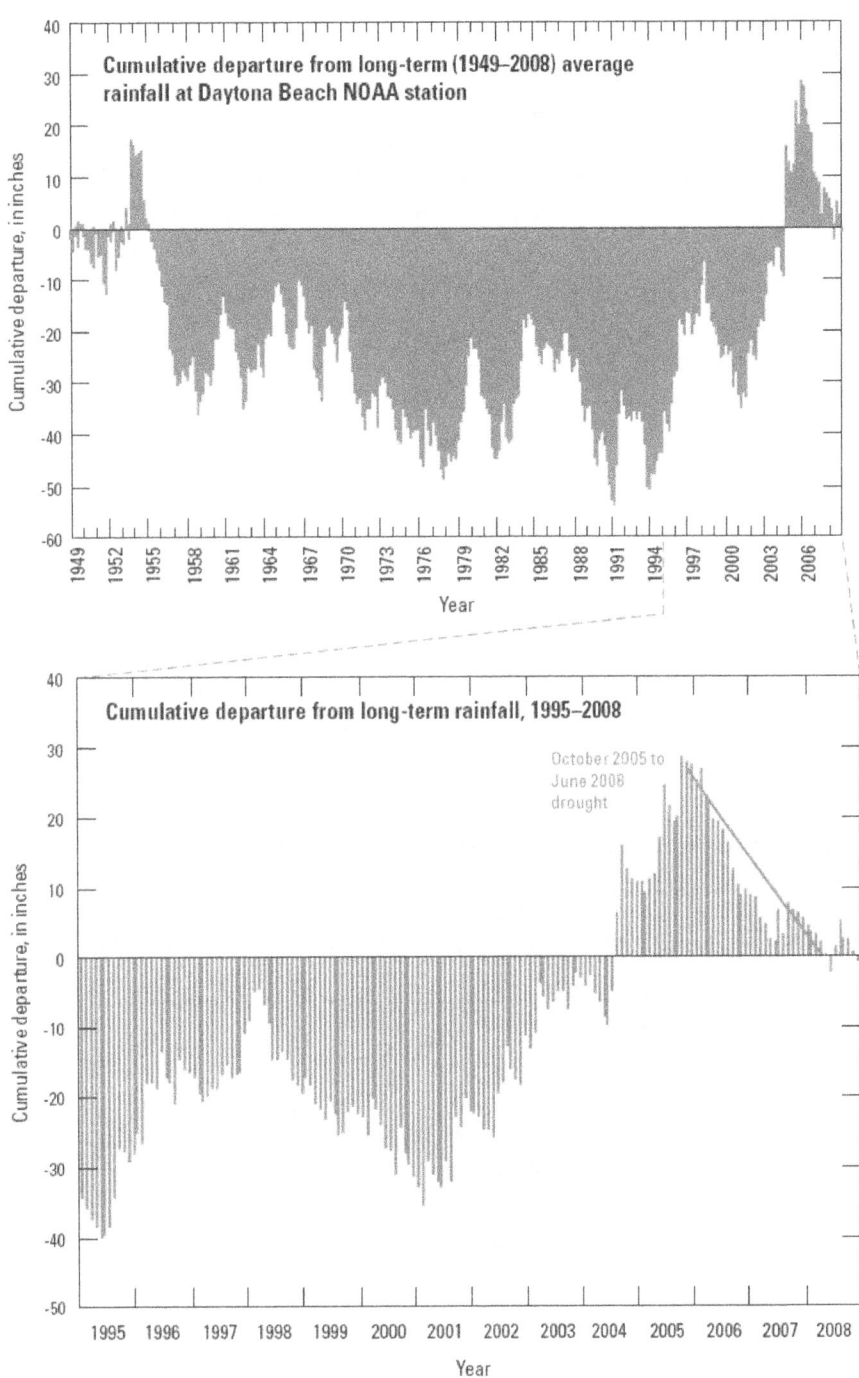

Figure 11. Cumulative departure of monthly rainfall from the long-term (1949–2008) average measured at the Daytona Beach National Oceanic and Atmospheric Administration rainfall station, 1995–2008.

Table 10a. Regression equations chosen to model water-level changes at selected groundwater and lake monitoring sites during the drought of October 2005–June 2008.

[UFA, Upper Floridan aquifer; SAS, surficial aquifer system; VIF, variance inflation factor; D_L, Durbin statistic; R^2_{adj}, adjusted coefficient of determination; Mgal/d, million gallons per day; $prec_{2ma}$, 2-month moving average of precipitation, in inches; Q, monthly pumpage, in million gallons per day; Q_{2ma}, 2-month moving average of pumpage, in million gallons per day]

Project site	Average Q (Mgal/d)	Best regressed equation	VIF	D_L	R^2_{adj}
Tomoka SAS	30.3	$\Delta SAS = 2.19 + 0.251*prec_{2ma} - 0.105*Q_{2ma}$	1.00	1.73	0.68
Tomoka tower UFA	30.3	$\Delta UFA = 4.35 + 0.298*prec_{2ma} - 0.183*Q$	1.01	1.62	0.64
SR40 UFA	10.0	$\Delta UFA = -0.780 + 0.668*\ln(prec_{2ma})$	1.00	2.37	0.61
Union Camp SAS	21.2	$\Delta SAS = -1.58 + 0.487*prec_{2ma}$	1.00	2.09	0.51
Scoggin Lake	29.7	$\Delta WL = \exp(2.67 + 0.0068*prec_{2ma} - 0.0141*Q_{2ma}) - 10$	1.00	1.31	0.75
Indian Lake	32.0	$\Delta WL = 2.40 + 0.0675*prec_{2ma} - 0.0905*Q_{2ma}$	1.00	2.30	0.81

Table 10b. Computed p-values for explanatory variables associated with the regression equations in table 10a, October 2005–June 2008.

[UFA, Upper Floridan aquifer; SAS, surficial aquifer system; SIV, stressor influence value; $prec_{2ma}$, 2-month moving average of precipitation, in inches; Q, monthly pumpage, in million gallons per day; Q_{2ma}, 2-month moving average of pumpage, in million gallons per day; ns, not significant, given other terms in the model; Insuff. POR, site POR does not include full period of drought]

Project site	Explanatory variable in best regressed equation			SIV[1]
	$prec_{2ma}$	Q	Q_{2ma}	
Tiger Bay 4A UFA	Insuff. POR	Insuff. POR	Insuff. POR	
Tomoka tower SAS	<0.001	ns	0.015	2
Tomoka tower UFA	<0.001	0.002	ns	2
SR40 SAS	Insuff. POR	Insuff. POR	Insuff. POR	
SR40 UFA	<0.001	ns	ns	1
Indian Lake site 3 SAS	Insuff. POR	Insuff. POR	Insuff. POR	
Indian Lake 350 SAS	Insuff. POR	Insuff. POR	Insuff. POR	
Union Camp SAS	<0.001	ns	ns	1
Scoggin Lake	<0.001	ns	<0.001	3
Coon Pond	Insuff. POR	Insuff. POR	Insuff. POR	
Indian Lake	<0.001	ns	<0.001	3

[1]Explanation for stressor influence value (SIV) based on comparison of coefficient p-values.

1 Water-level changes are correlated with precipitation but not with pumpage.

2 Water-level changes are more highly correlated with precipitation than with pumpage.

3 Water-level changes are highly correlated with both precipitation and pumpage.

4 Water-level changes are more highly correlated with pumpage than with precipitation.

5 Water-level changes are correlated with pumpage but not with precipitation.

Table 11. Comparison of results from multiple linear regression analyses.

[insuff. POR, insufficient period of record]

Project site	Available period of record		Results for available POR	Results for May 2000 to June 2007	Seasonal analyses (applied across available POR)				Drought analyses October 2005 to June 2008	Average SIV[5]
	From	To			Winter[1]	Spring[2]	Summer[3]	Fall[4]		
					Stressor influence value, SIV[5]					
Tiger Bay 4A UFA	Sep-97	Jun-07	3	3	1	3	2	3	insuff. POR	
Tokoma tower SAS	Jun-03	Dec-08	2	insuff. POR	insuff. POR	insuff. POR	insuff. POR	insuff. POR	2	
Tokoma tower UFA	Jan-95	Dec-08	3	3	3	2	1	3	2	2.4
SR40 SAS	Jan-95	Dec-07	1	1	1	1	1	2	insuff. POR	
SR40 UFA	Jan-95	Dec-08	1	1	1	1	2	2	1	1.3
Indian Lk site 3 SAS	Nov-05	Dec-08	2	insuff. POR	insuff. POR	insuff. POR	insuff. POR	insuff. POR	insuff. POR	
Indian Lk 350 SAS	Jan-95	Dec-04	1	insuff. POR	1	2	1	5	insuff. POR	
Union Camp SAS	Jan-95	Apr-08	2	2	1	1	2	2	1	1.6
Scoggin Lake	May-05	Dec-08	3	2	insuff. POR	insuff. POR	insuff. POR	insuff. POR	3	
Coon Pond	Sep-01	Aug-08	1	insuff. POR	insuff. POR	insuff. POR	insuff. POR	insuff. POR	insuff. POR	
Indian Lake	Jul-99	Dec-08	3	3	insuff. POR	insuff. POR	insuff. POR	insuff. POR	3	
Average SIV[5] ———			2.0	2.1	1 3	1.7	1.5	2.8	2.0	
					Adjusted coefficient of determination, R^2_{adj}					Average R^2_{adj}
Tiger Bay 4A UFA	Sep-97	Jun-07	0.64	0.66	0.43	0.62	0.58	0.83	insuff. POR	
Tokoma tower SAS	Jun-03	Dec-08	0.81	insuff. POR	insuff. POR	insuff. POR	insuff. POR	insuff. POR	0.68	
Tokoma tower UFA	Jan-95	Dec-08	0.60	0.60	0.55	0.67	0.46	0 50	0.64	0.57
SR40 SAS	Jan-95	Dec-07	0.61	0.66	0.53	0.48	0.63	0.73	insuff. POR	
SR40 UFA	Jan-95	Dec-08	0.45	0.40	0.09	0.52	0.76	0.71	0.61	0.51
Indian Lk site 3 SAS	Nov-05	Dec-08	0.62	insuff. POR	insuff. POR	insuff. POR	insuff. POR	insuff. POR	insuff. POR	
Indian Lk 350 SAS	Jan-95	Dec-04	0.45	insuff. POR	0.80	0.55	0.36	0.40	insuff. POR	
Union Camp SAS	Jan-95	Apr-08	0.43	0.43	0.26	0.44	0.55	0.46	0.51	0.44
Scoggin Lake	May-05	Dec-08	0.41	0.46	insuff. POR	insuff. POR	insuff. POR	insuff. POR	0.75	
Coon Pond	Sep-01	Aug-08	0.70	insuff. POR	insuff. POR	insuff. POR	insuff. POR	insuff. POR	insuff. POR	
Indian Lake	Jul-99	Dec-08	0.70	0.73	insuff. POR	insuff. POR	insuff. POR	insuff. POR	0.81	
Average R^2_{adj} ———			0.58	0.56	0.44	0.55	0.56	0.61	0.67	

[1]December, January, and February.

[2]March, April, and May.

[3]June, July, August.

[4]September, October, and November.

[5]Explanation for stressor influence value (SIV) based on comparison of coefficient p-values.

1   Water-level changes are correlated with precipitation but not with pumpage.

2   Water-level changes are more highly correlated with precipitation than with pumpage.

3   Water-level changes are highly correlated with both precipitation and pumpage.

4   Water-level changes are more highly correlated with pumpage than with precipitation.

5   Water-level changes are correlated with pumpage but not with precipitation

Regional Effects of Groundwater Withdrawals

The SIV and R^2_{adj} values documented thus far account for groundwater withdrawals aggregated from all of the pumping wells located within 12 mi of the project sites. This was done to account for the collective influence of all of the principal well fields in north Volusia County. For a given withdrawal rate, pumping wells (or well fields) located closer to the monitoring sites would be expected to a have greater influence on water levels than wells located at greater distances. Accordingly, the analyses discussed below examine how the relations between precipitation, groundwater withdrawals, and water-level changes are affected if withdrawals are aggregated at varying distances of less than 12 mi from the project sites. That is, regressions were conducted to account for pumping rates aggregated from wells located within 1, 2, 3, 4, 5, 6, 7, 8, and 10 mi of the sites (nine analyses per site). Aggregated pumping rates for these increasing radial distances

are shown on figure 7. The SIV and R^2_{adj} values determined from each of these nine analyses were compared with those previously documented in table 6b to determine if relations between the explanatory and response variables had changed. Only those six sites previously found to be correlated with groundwater withdrawals summed within the 12-mi distances (that is, sites having SIVs of 2 or greater as listed in table 6b), and which were located within a mile of the nearest pumping well, were included in these analyses.

Accounting for radially dependent increases in cumulative groundwater withdrawals did not affect the relations between water-level changes and withdrawals at any of the six sites (table 12). That is, accounting for withdrawals from pumping wells aggregated at distances of less than 12 mi of each site produced the same SIV as that determined for the withdrawal rate aggregated within 12 mi of the site. Also, increases in cumulative withdrawals had relatively little effect on R^2_{adj} values (fig. 12).

Table 12.   Stressor influence values determined for regression models using groundwater withdrawals aggregated over varying distances from the project sites.

[UFA, Upper Floridan aquifer; SAS, surficial aquifer system; $\leq$, less than or equal to; *prec*, monthly precipitation, in inches; $prec_{2ma}$, 2-month moving average of *prec*, in inches; $\Delta prec_{2ma}$, 2-month moving average of change in *prec*, in inches; *pet*, monthly potential evapotranspiration, in inches; $(p\text{-}pet)_{2ma}$, 2-month moving average of the difference between *prec* and *pet*, in inches; Q_{2ma}, 2-month moving average of pumpage, in million gallons per day; ΔQ, monthly change in pumpage, in million gallons per day; ΔQ_{2ma}, 2-month moving average of change in pumpage, in million gallons per day; np, no pumpage located within indicated distance of site. Available periods of record used in analyses are shown in table 1]

Project site and variables in best regressed equations	Distance from project site, in miles									
	≤ 1	≤ 2	≤ 3	≤ 4	≤ 5	≤ 6	≤ 7	≤ 8	≤ 10	≤ 12
	Stressor Influence Value (SIV)[1]									
Tiger Bay 4A UFA										
$\Delta prec_{2ma}$, $(p\text{-}pet)_{2ma}$, ΔQ	3	3	3	3	3	3	3	3	3	3
Tomoka tower SAS										
$prec_{2ma}$, $\Delta prec_{2ma}$, Q_{2ma}	2	2	2	2	2	2	2	2	2	2
Tomoka tower UFA										
$prec_{2ma}$, ΔQ_{2ma}	3	3	3	3	3	3	3	3	3	3
Indian Lake site 3 SAS										
$prec_{2ma}$, Q_{2ma}	2	2	2	2	2	2	2	2	2	2
Indian Lake										
$prec_{2ma}$, Q_{2ma}	3	3	3	3	3	3	3	3	3	3
PZ-A										
$prec_{2ma}$, $\Delta prec_{2ma}$, Q	2	2	2	2	2	2	2	2	2	2

[1]Explanation for stressor influence value (SIV) based on comparison of coefficient p-values.

1   Water-level changes are correlated with precipitation but not with pumpage.

2   Water-level changes are more highly correlated with precipitation than with pumpage.

3   Water-level changes are highly correlated with both precipitation and pumpage.

4   Water-level changes are more highly correlated with pumpage than with precipitation.

5   Water-level changes are correlated with pumpage but not with precipitation

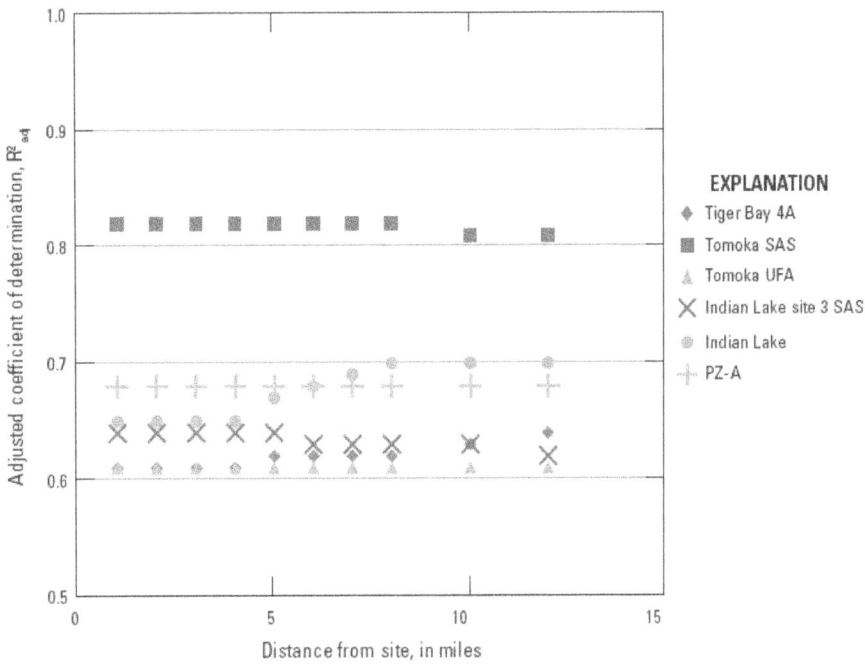

Figure 12.   Adjusted coefficient of determination versus varying distances from the project sites.

Sources of Error in Regression Models

Environmental regression models inherently contain some level of unexplained noise or error (the "e" term in eq. 1). The R^2_{adj} statistics documented in this report indicate that 9 to 83 percent of the variance in the response variable was accounted for by the models. Conversely, 17 to 91 percent of the variance could not be explained by these models. This error can be attributed to a combination of factors including data measurement errors, failure to consider unrecognized but pertinent explanatory variables, and violations of model assumptions, such as nonlinear regression coefficients and nonnormal distribution and heteroscedasticity of residuals.

Data-related errors may include inaccuracies in measured water levels, water-use rates, and precipitation. Actual evapotranspiration is a superior parameter to PET for analyzing SAS water-level changes, because it provides a more accurate estimate of water lost from the system, and thus of water availability, when subtracted from precipitation. Related errors would be more problematic at the groundwater sites, where the water table may be up to several feet below land surface during drier parts of the year, than at the lake sites where the open water surface provides an unlimited source of evaporative supply. Unfortunately, estimation of actual evapotranspiration rates required information on additional input variables that was not readily available for this study.

Exclusion of explanatory variables, such as groundwater withdrawal for agricultural use, may have affected results at

some sites, particularly those nearest areas of concentrated usage such as SR40 SAS and SR40 UFA. The effects of these withdrawals would be most pronounced during the winter months when withdrawals for freeze protection can be substantial. Omission of agricultural withdrawals may thus help to explain the low R^2_{adj} value (0.09) determined at SR40 UFA during the winter months (table 9a). Other factors not considered in these analyses that could potentially affect water levels include land-use modifications, such as changes in impervious covers, ditching, canals, and other drainage modifications.

Errors can be introduced by use of a monthly, as opposed to a daily, time-averaging period. Monthly averaged data can mute the response of water-level changes to precipitation events or miss them altogether. Also, the approach used here of dividing a well field's total withdrawal equally among contributing production wells, as opposed to assigning each well its true rate, may be problematic, particularly if larger-capacity wells are located relatively close to monitored sites.

Finally, it is important to note that the results documented in this report (explanatory variables included in regression models, SIVs, and R^2_{adj} values) apply to those specific criteria used in selecting the best regressed equations. These criteria include a significance level of 0.05 for screening explanatory variables, restricting best regressed equations to a maximum of three explanatory variables, and excluding results having VIF values of greater than 2.0. Other selection criteria may affect the outcome of these regression statistics.

Analyses of Discharge at Tiger Bay Canal

Discharge measured at the Tiger Bay canal between 1978 and 2001 was analyzed using flow-duration and double-mass curves, trend analyses, and hypothesis testing. These analyses were intended to determine if canal discharge measured prior to full development of the nearby well field (1978 to 1988) is statistically different from measured conditions following well field development (1989 to 2001). If differences were identified, analyses were used to determine if some factor(s) other than precipitation may have contributed to the change.

Flow-duration curves depicted in figure 13 indicate that discharge at Tiger Bay, especially during base-flow conditions, is greater between 1978 to 1988 than between 1989 and 2001. For example, a daily discharge of 0.1 ft³/s was equaled or exceeded about 70 percent of the time during the first 11-year period, but only about 50 percent of the time over the latter 13-year period. These hydrologic analyses do not provide information regarding causative factors for reductions in flow.

Several statistical tests were conducted to compare low-flow characteristics between the two periods and evaluate whether some factor(s) other than rainfall is (are) responsible for the differences. One approach is to examine changes in a test metric, such as the number of zero-flow days, which can be associated with low-flow conditions. Between 1978 and 1988, an annual median of 100 zero-flow days was measured at the site, considerably less than the median of 190 days between 1989 and 2001 (fig. 14). Median annual precipitation, however, was virtually equal between the two periods (46.7 in. from 1978 to 1988 and 46.4 in. from 1989 and 2001). Although a

Mann-Whitney test indicates that a statistically significant difference exists between the two median values of zero-flow days (p-value of 0.027), no such significant difference was found between the two median precipitation values (p-value of 0.99). Similarly, a two-sample t-test determined that the difference between the mean annual numbers of zero-flow days between the two periods was also significant, even though the difference between mean annual precipitation was not significant (plots of these t-test results are not shown). The parametric t-test was deemed appropriate for this application, given that a Kolmogrov-Smirnov test (Conover, 1999) verified that the annual means were normally distributed. Both of these hypothesis tests indicate that some factor other than precipitation contributed to a significant decrease in the number of zero-flow days observed between the two periods corresponding to pre- and post- well-field operations.

The number of zero-flow days measured annually between 1978 and 2001, as well as annual precipitation, were analyzed for trends using the nonparametric Kendall test (Helsel and Hirsch, 2002). By including the entire POR, the analyses accounts for the period of time when both the southern and northern parts of the nearby well field were being developed. As shown in figure 15, the slope of the Theil-Kendall line of best fit is significantly greater than zero (p-value of 0.014), indicating a significant increasing trend in the number of zero-flow days between 1978 and 2001. Conversely, no significant trend was found in annual precipitation (p-value = 0.80), again indicating that some factor(s) other than rainfall was (were) responsible for increases in the number of zero-flow days over the 24-year period.

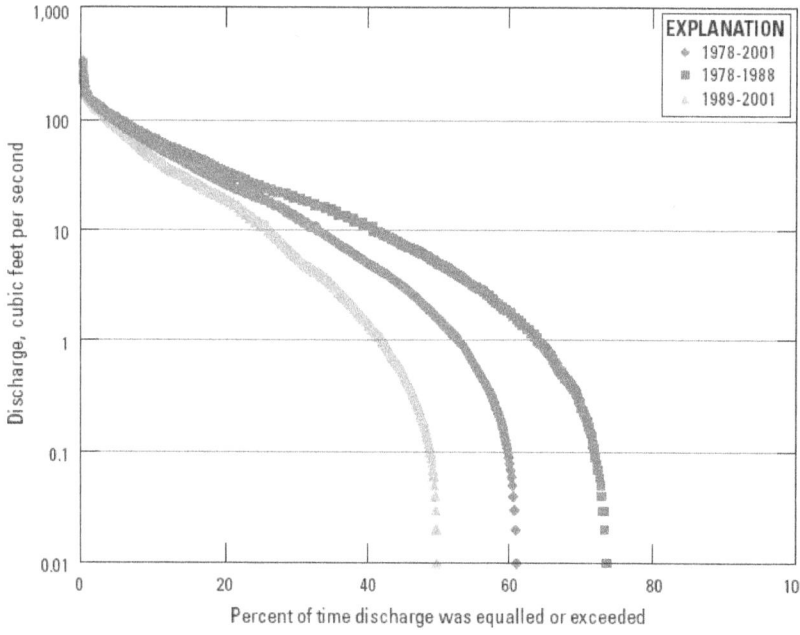

Figure 13.   Flow duration curves of discharge at the Tiger Bay canal, 1978–2001.

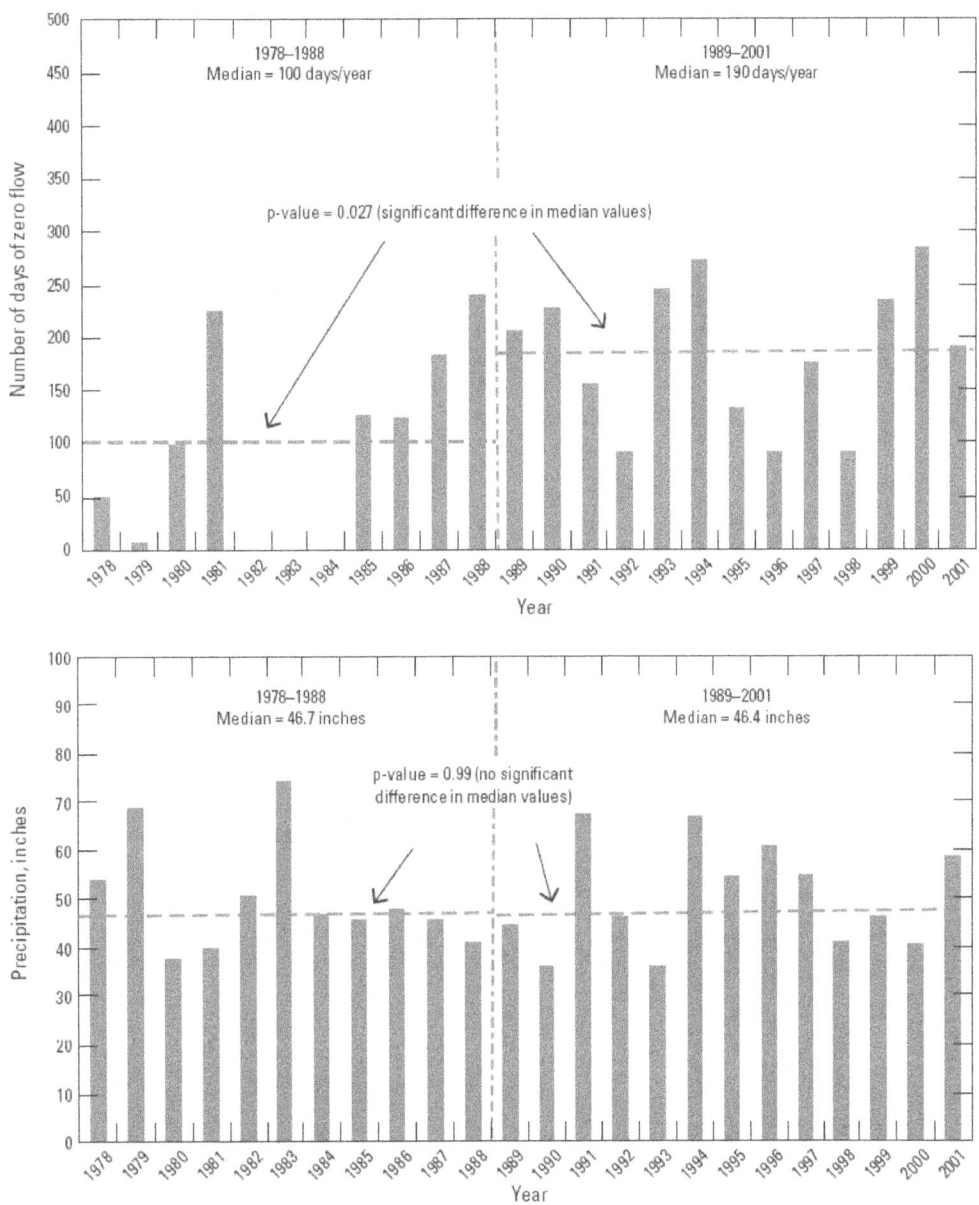

Figure 14.   Results of a Mann-Whitney analyses of the number of days of zero flow at Tiger Bay canal and precipitation at the Daytona Beach National Oceanic and Atmospheric Administration rainfall station, 1978–2001.

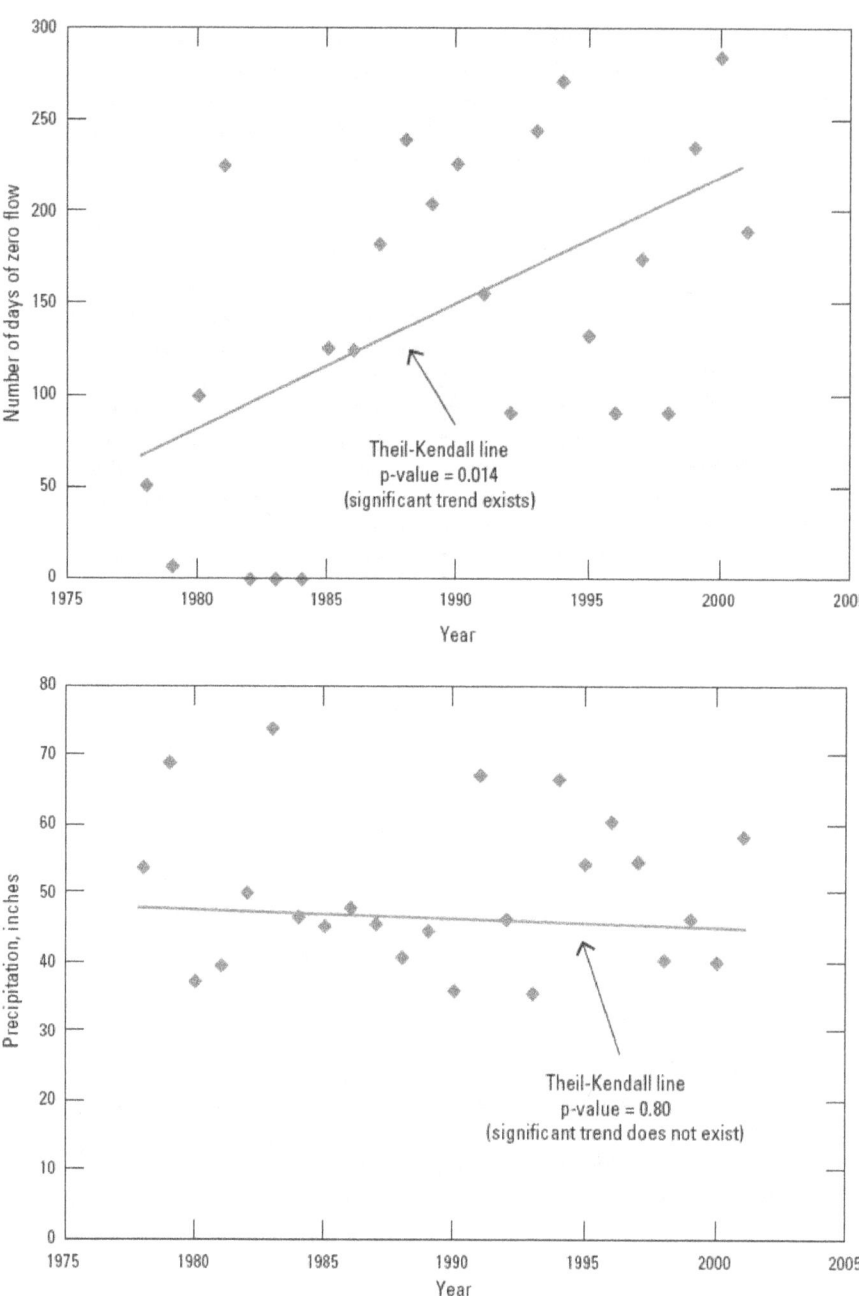

Figure 15. Results of trend analyses of the number of days of zero flow at the Tiger Bay canal and precipitation at the Daytona Beach National Oceanic and Atmospheric Administration rainfall station, 1978–2001.

Cumulative discharge at Tiger Bay was plotted against cumulative discharge measured at the USGS site on the Tomoka River near Holly Hill (fig. 16). The Tomoka River is located about 5 mi northeast of Tiger Bay and presumably would be unaffected by pumping from the Indian Lake Road well field or by any other anthropogenic factor that may have contributed to decreases in the number of zero-flow days at Tiger Bay. The double-mass relation remains constant from 1978 to about 1988, after which the slope flattens to indicate a reduction in discharge at Tiger Bay relative to that at Tomoka River. The break in the curve occurs at about the same time (1988) when the well field was reported to be fully operational. Assuming that annual precipitation was about the same at the Tiger Bay and Tomoka River sites, the change in slope can be attributed to some other factor(s) that served to reduce the discharge at Tiger Bay or to increase the discharge at Tomoka River in 1988.

To determine which of these two possible explanations is valid, the 2-year moving average of precipitation at the Daytona Beach NOAA station was plotted against the number of zero-flow days at Tiger Bay and against the number of days having flow rates of less than or equal to 4.7 ft^3/s at Tomoka River (fig. 17). Using a 2-year moving average of precipitation smooth the data to make relations with flow more discernible. A discharge of 4.7 ft^3/s was selected for use in the Tomoka plot to allow for comparison of a common flow metric between the two sites; that is, flows of 4.7 and 0 ft^3/s represent the first quartile flow statistic for the Tomoka River and Tiger Bay sites, respectively. The data plotted in figure 17 are color coded to distinguish between the two periods of interest. At Tiger Bay, even though points between the two periods are scattered and overlap in some cases, the data appear to show that, for a given 2-year moving average of precipitation, the period between 1989 and 2001 can be associated with a greater number of zero flow days than can the period between 1978 and 1988. In contrast, the Tomoka River data are more intermixed across the two periods with relatively little separation between the regressed lines of best fit. When applied to these data, the Mann-Whitney test indicated that no significant difference exists between median discharges measured across the two periods at the Tomoka River site (p-value of 0.99). In addition, a Kendall test detected no significant trend in the number of days having flows of less than or equal to 4.7 ft^3/s across the 24-year POR at Tomoka (p-value of 0.88). Based on these results, the break in slope shown in figure 16 can be attributed to a reduction in Tiger Bay discharge caused by some factor(s) other than precipitation.

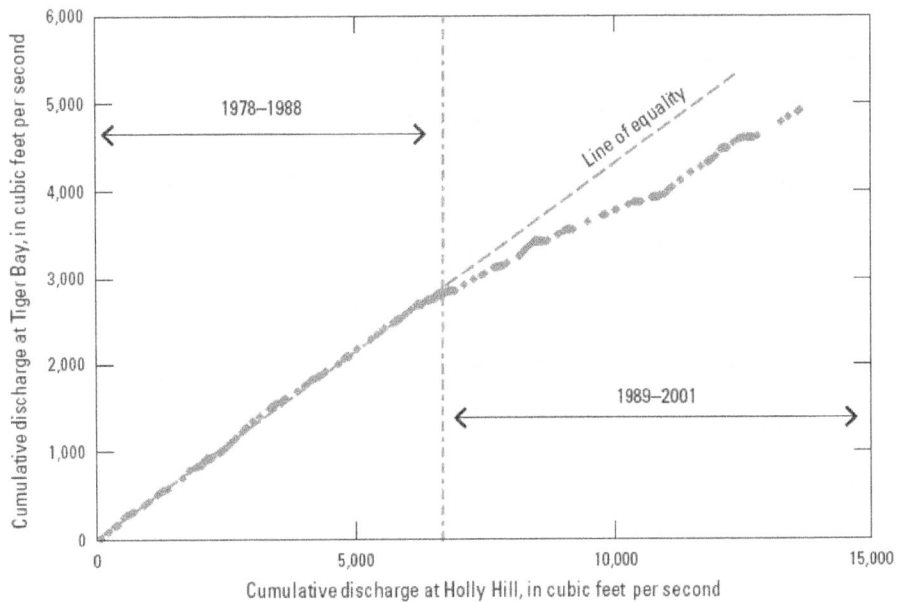

Figure 16. Cumulative discharge at Tiger Bay canal (USGS site 02247480) versus cumulative discharge at Tomoka River near Holly Hill, 1978–2001.

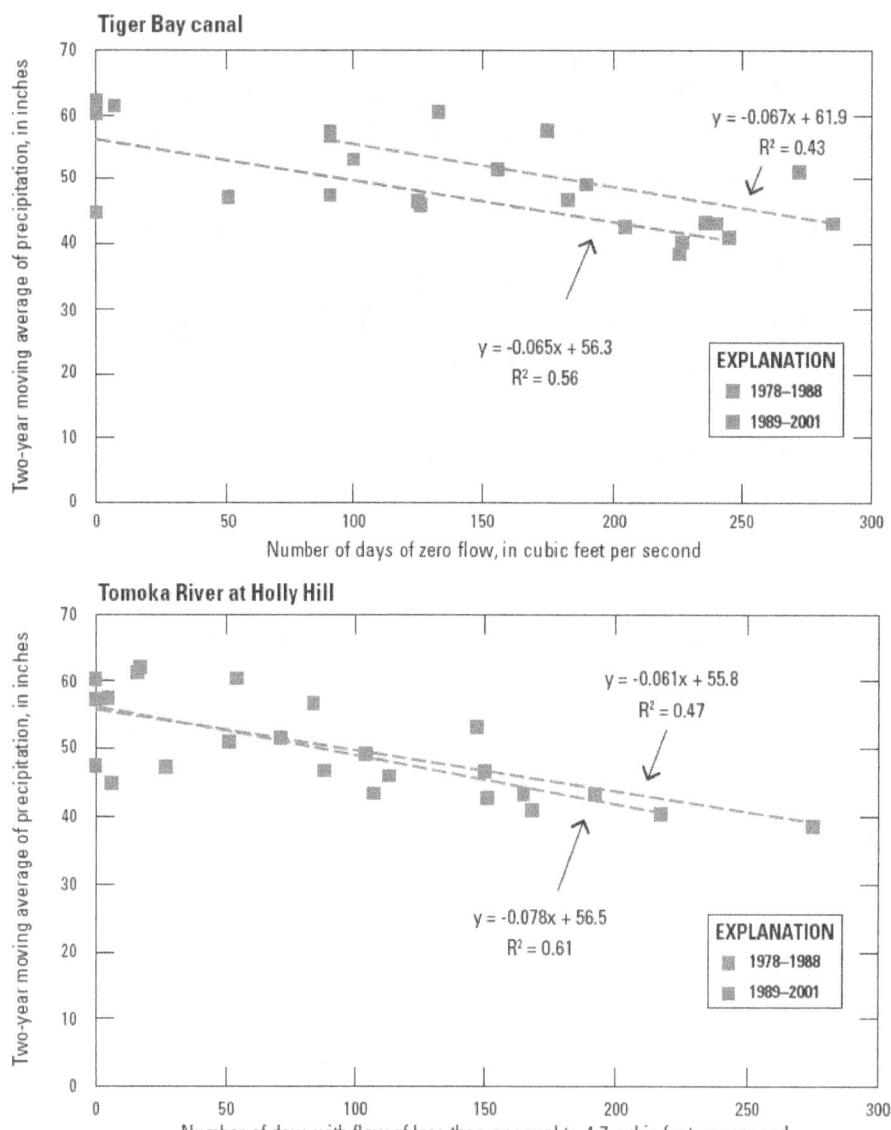

Figure 17.   The 2-year moving average of precipitation at the Daytona Beach National Oceanic and Atmospheric Administration rainfall station versus the number of days of zero flow in the Tiger Bay canal and flows of less than or equal to 4.7 cubic feet per second at the Tomoka River site, 1978–2001.

Summary and Conclusions

Volusia County is located in east-central Florida and comprises about 1,200 square miles which includes the coastal communities of Daytona Beach, Ormond Beach, and New Smyrna Beach. Groundwater used to meet the County's municipal, agricultural, and commercial needs is pumped from the Upper Floridan aquifer (UFA), a semiconfined sequence of highly transmissive carbonate rocks. Withdrawals from this aquifer not only lower the aquifer's water level, which can reduce the amounts of groundwater discharged from UFA springs and laterally to the ocean, but also can lower water levels in the overlying unconfined surficial aquifer system (SAS). Lowered SAS water levels, in turn, can affect other sensitive water resources, such as wetlands and associated ecosystems. In addition to groundwater withdrawals, natural meteorological fluctuations in precipitation and evapotranspiration influence groundwater levels and affect water resources; however, often it is not apparent how these factors contribute to changes in SAS and UFA water levels. Consequently, trends and fluctuations observed in hydrologic data reflect the combined effects of climatic and anthropogenic influences and thus pose difficulties for water managers tasked with assessing the effects of new groundwater-use permits in resource-sensitive areas, or of implementing water-use restrictions during periods of drought.

Multiple linear regression analyses were conducted to assess the relative influences of precipitation and groundwater withdrawals on monthly changes in groundwater and lake levels at selected monitoring sites within a wetland area of north-central Volusia County. Streamflow data collected at the USGS Tiger Bay canal gaging station between 1978 and 2001 were analyzed using flow-duration and double-mass curves, trend analyses, and hypothesis testing to contrast flow conditions prior and subsequent to development of a nearby municipal well field. Water-level data collected by the St. Johns River Water Management District at 17 groundwater sites and 3 lake sites were analyzed across varying periods of record (PORs) between 1995 and 2010 to account for varying climatic and anthropogenic conditions. Groundwater withdrawals from municipal water-supply wells located within 12 miles (mi) of the sites were summed to collectively account for well fields in northern Volusia County. Precipitation and the difference between precipitation and PET, a gross estimate of the minimum amount of water available to recharge the SAS, were included as explanatory variables in the analyses. Regressions were conducted across (1) available PORs to maximize the number of observations and account for precipitation-averaged conditions; (2) May 2000 to June 2007 to allow for comparison of individual site results across a common period of record; (3) individual seasons to examine relations between water levels and varying stressor conditions; and (4) an extended period of drought (October 2005 to June 2008) to contrast relations with those determined across precipitation-averaged PORs. Finally, analyses were performed to examine how the relations between the response

and explanatory variables were affected by accounting for groundwater withdrawals aggregated within less than 12 mi from the sites.

As an analytical tool, MLR analyses provided results consistent with the locations and targeted aquifer monitoring zones of the project wells. That is, water-level changes tended to be less influenced by groundwater withdrawal at sites farther away from municipal well fields than at sites closer to well fields. Also, water-level changes measured in UFA monitoring wells tended to be more highly correlated with groundwater withdrawals than did changes in SAS levels, which were more highly (or solely) correlated with precipitation. However, water-level changes predicted by the regression models underestimated measured changes across precipitation-averaged PORs for observations having large positive monthly water-level changes (generally greater than 1.0 foot). Such observations are associated with high precipitation and were identified as points in the regression analyses that produced large standardized residuals and/or observations of high leverage. Thus, regression models produced by multiple linear regression (MLR) analyses may have better predictive capability in wetland environments when applied to periods of average (or drought like) climatic conditions than for wetter conditions.

Regressions accounted for 9 to 83 percent of the variance in water-level changes across the four sets of analyses. Water-level changes tended to be more highly correlated with precipitation than with groundwater withdrawals, particularly across PORs having precipitation-averaged conditions. Climatic variables most frequently correlated with water-level changes in the regression models included the 2-month moving averages of precipitation and change in precipitation, whereas the 2-month moving averages of groundwater withdrawals and change in withdrawal were included as common anthropogenic variables. These results indicate that water-level changes in both aquifer systems are not only influenced by current monthly climatic and anthropogenic conditions, but also by those of the previous month.

The relations between explanatory variables and stage changes at Indian and Scoggin Lakes were more comparable to those determined for the UFA sites than for the SAS sites. That is, water-level changes at both the lake and UFA sites tended to be more highly correlated with groundwater withdrawals than were changes at SAS sites, which indicates that the lakes may be better connected hydraulically to the UFA than the SAS is at nearby sites. A previous seismic-reflection profiling study conducted by the USGS at Indian Lake identified two distinct subsurface collapse features beneath the lake that may be providing preferential flow paths for groundwater moving between the two aquifers.

The relations between changes in water levels, precipitation, and groundwater withdrawals are dynamic and vary seasonally. Water-level changes tended to be most highly correlated with withdrawals during the spring when increases in monthly withdrawal rates contributed to water-level declines and during the fall when reduced withdrawal rates contributed to recovery of water levels. Conversely, changes in water levels tended to be most highly (or solely) correlated with precipitation in the winter when withdrawals were minimized and in the summer when precipitation was greatest. Potential evapotranspiration was best related with water-level changes during the spring months, which tend to be warm and dry. Seasonal R^2_{adj} values ranged from 0.83 at Tiger Bay 4A UFA (fall) to 0.09 at SR40 UFA (winter). The high degree of unexplained error at SR40 UFA may be due, in part, to the effects of short-lived but high rates of groundwater withdrawals needed for freeze protection of agricultural crops in the winter months, a stress not accounted for in the analyses.

Water-level changes measured during the drought of October 2005 to June 2008 were more highly correlated with groundwater withdrawal at sites located near municipal well fields (Tomoka tower SAS and UFA) than at sites further removed from withdrawals (SR40 UFA and Union Camp SAS). These relations are similar to those found for precipitation-averaged PORs. Water-level changes at Indian and Scoggin Lakes were more highly correlated with groundwater withdrawals during the drought than were nearby changes in the SAS. Drought-induced pumping rates were, on average, greater than those for precipitation-averaged conditions. The relatively high values of R^2_{adj} (0.81 and 0.75) determined for Indian and Scoggin Lakes indicate that drought-induced changes in stage were well explained by the variables included in the best regressed equations. When compared with results generated across precipitation-averaged PORs, analyses of drought conditions markedly improved results at both lakes. Surface-water runoff, which contributed water to the lakes during the wetter periods included within the available PORs, possibly introduced some degree of nonlinearity and/or unexplained error in the relations between stage and precipitation. The absence of surface runoff during periods of drought, however, may help to minimize such error.

Accounting for radially dependent increases in aggregated groundwater withdrawals did not affect the relation between water-level changes and withdrawals at any the six sites included in the analyses. That is, accounting for withdrawals aggregated within varying distances of less than 12 mi of the sites produced virtually the same relations as those determined for withdrawals summed within 12 mi of the site. Increases in aggregated groundwater withdrawals had relatively little effect on R^2_{adj} values.

Analyses of streamflow at the gaged site on the Tiger Bay canal indicate that significant reductions have occurred in the number of zero-flow days between the periods of 1978 to 1988 and 1989 to 2001. These periods coincide with conditions prior and subsequent to development of a nearby municipal well field. Flow-duration curves indicate that discharge at Tiger Bay, especially during base- flow conditions, was greater between 1978 to 1988 than between 1989 and 2001. Mann-Whitney and two-sample t tests indicated that, although significant differences exists in the median and mean number of zero-flow days between the two periods, no such differences exist in respective precipitation values. Similarly,

Kendall trend tests indicated that, although a significant positive trend exists in the number of zero-flow days over the 24-year period, no such trend was found in precipitation. Finally, a break in the slope of a double-mass curve plotting the discharge at Tiger Bay versus the discharge at the USGS site on the Tomoka River (located about 5 mi from the Tiger Bay site) indicated a reduction in the discharge at Tiger Bay. This reduction occurred at about the same time (1988 to 1989) when the nearby well field became fully operational. Collectively, these results show that changes in flow conditions, particularly low-flow conditions, between the two periods of interest can be attributed to some factor (or factors) other than rainfall.

Selected References

Bush, P.W., 1978, Hydrologic evaluation of part of central Volusia County, Florida: U.S. Geological Survey Open-File Report 78–89, 50 p.

Conover, W.L., 1999, Practical nonparametric statistics, (3d ed.): New York, John Wiley, 584 p.

Cunningham, K.J., and Walker, C., 2009, Seismic-sag structural systems in the Tertiary carbonate rocks beneath southeastern Florida, USA: Evidence for hypogenic speleogenesis? *in* Hypogene Speleogenesis and Karst Hydrogeology of Artesian Basins: Ukrainian Institute of Speleology and Karstology, Special Paper 1, p. 151–158.

Durbin, J., and Watson, G.S., 1951, Testing for serial correlation in least squares regression II: Biometrika, v. 38.

Helsel, D.R., and Hirsch, R.M., 2002, Statistical methods in water resources: U.S. Geological Survey, Techniques of Water-Resources Investigations, book 4, chap. A3, 510 p.

Kindinger, J.L., Davis, J.B., and Flocks, J.G., 2000, Subsurface characterization of selected water bodies in the St. Johns River Water Management District, northeast Florida: U.S. Geological Survey Open-File Report 00–180, 24 p.

Lopez, M.A., and Fretwell, J.D., 1992, Relation of change in water levels in surficial and Upper Floridan aquifers and lake stage to climatic conditions and well-field pumpage in northwest Hillsborough, northeast Pinellas, and south Pasco Counties, Florida: U.S. Geological Survey Water-Resources Investigations Report 91–4158, 94 p.

Montgomery, D.C., and Peck, E.A., 1982, Introduction to linear regression analysis: New York, John Wiley, 504 p.

Murray, L.C., Jr., 2010, Relations between groundwater levels and anthropogenic and meteorological stressors at selected sites in east-central Florida: U.S. Geological Survey Scientific Investigations Report 2010–046, 31 p.

Murray, L.C., Jr., and Halford, K.J., 1996, Hydrogeologic conditions and simulation of ground-water flow in the greater Orlando metropolitan area, east-central Florida: U.S. Geological Survey Water-Resources Investigations Report 96–4181, 100 p.

Priestley, C.B., and Taylor, R.J., 1972, On the assessment of surface heat flux and evaporation using large-scale parameters: Monthly Weather Review 100, p. 81–92.

Riekerk, H., and Korhnak, L.V., 2000, The hydrology of cypress wetlands in Florida pine flatwoods: Wetlands, v. 20, no. 3, p. 448–460.

Rutledge, A.T., 1984, Use of double-mass curves to determine drawdown in a long-term aquifer test in north-central Volusia County, Florida: U.S. Geological Survey Water-Resources Investigations Report 84–4309, 29 p.

Searcy, J.K., and Hardison, C.H., 1960, Double-mass curves; *with a section on* Fitting curves to cyclic data, *in* Manual of Hydrology: Part 1. General surface-water techniques: U.S. Geological Survey Water-Supply Paper 1541–B, 66 p.

Searcy, J.K., 1959, Flow-duration curves, *in* Manual of Hydrology: Part 2. Low-flow techniques: U.S. Geological Survey Water-Supply Paper 1542–A, 33 p.

Sumner, D.M., 2001, Evapotranspiration from a cypress and pine forest subjected to natural fires, Volusia County, Florida, 1998–99: U.S. Geological Survey Water-Resources Investigations Report 01–4245, 56 p.

Tibbals, C.H., 1990, Hydrology of the Floridan aquifer system in east-central Florida: U.S. Geological Survey Professional Paper 1403–E, 98 p.

Turnipseed, D.P., and Sauer, V.B., 2010, Discharge measurements at gaging stations: U.S. Geological Survey Techniques and Methods 3–A8, 87 p.

U.S. Geological Survey, 2009, Florida Water Science Center Hydrologic Data Portal: Available at *http://hdwp.er.usgs.gov.*

U.S. Geological Survey, 2001, Water Resources Data, Florida Water Year 2001: Volume 1A. Northeast Florida Surface Water, Water-Data Report FL–01–1A, 398 p.

Watts, K.R., 1995, Regression models of monthly water level change in and near the closed basin division of the San Luis Valley, south-central Colorado: U.S. Geological Survey Water-Resources Investigations Report 96–4181, 100 p.

Wyrick, G.G., 1960, The ground-water resources of Volusia County, Florida: Florida Geological Survey Report of Investigations 22, 65 p.